D1483189

THE INVADER OF HIS COUNTRY
OR THE FATAL RESENTMENT

BY JOHN DENNIS

1720

A FACSIMILE PUBLISHED BY CORNMARKET PRESS
FROM THE COPY IN THE BIRMINGHAM SHAKESPEARE LIBRARY
LONDON
1969

PUBLISHED BY CORNMARKET PRESS LIMITED
42/43 CONDUIT STREET LONDON W1R ONL
PRINTED IN ENGLAND BY FLETCHER AND SON LIMITED NORWICH

SBN 7191 0115 8

THE

INVADER of His Country:

OR,

The Fatal Resentment.

A

TRAGEDY.

As it is Acted at the

Theatre-Royal in *Drury-Lane.*

By His MAJESTY's Servants.

By Mr. DENNIS.

LONDON:

Printed for *J. Pemberton* in *Fleet-street,* and *J. Watts* near *Lincolns-Inn-Fields*: And Sold by *J. Brotherton* and *W. Meadows* in *Cornhill*; *T. Jauncy* and *A. Dodd* without *Temple-Bar*; *W. Lewis* in *Covent-Garden,* and *J. Graves* at *St. James's.* 1720.   [Price 1 *s* 6 *d.*]

To His Grace

THOMAS,

Duke of *Newcastle*,

Lord Chamberlain of His MAJESTY's
Houshold, one of His MAJESTY's *most
Honourable Privy-Council, and Knight
of the most Noble Order of the Garter.*

My LORD,

I Take the Liberty to Dedi-
cate to Your GRACE *The
Invader of his Country,*
which is the *Coriolanus* of
Shakespear alter'd by me.
And I have presum'd to do
this without asking Your
Leave, because this is a Dedication of an extraordina-
ry Nature, and an Application to Your GRACE
for Justice, in a Cause that is determinable by
Your GRACE alone, by vertue of Your Office;
as all Causes of the like Nature, ever since I

A 2   could

DEDICATION.

could remember, have been decided in the laſt Appeal by Your GRACE's Predeceſſors.

My LORD, *Coriolanus* throws himſelf at Your GRACE's Feet, in order to obtain Juſtice of You, after having received as injurious Treatment from the petulant Deportment of two or three Inſolent Players, as ever he formerly did at *Rome* from the Brutal Rage of the Rabble. He has been baniſh'd from our Theatre by the one, thro' a miſtaken Greedineſs of Gain, as the other formerly expell'd him from *Rome* thro' a groundleſs Jealouſy of Power.

My LORD, when I tell the World that *Coriolanus* has been unjuſtly baniſh'd from our Theatre by two or three Inſolent Players, I am ſure all thoſe will be apt to believe me, who will reflect with Indignation and Diſdain, that that *Roman* is not the firſt Nobleman whom they have audaciouſly dar'd to exclude from thence. And I hope this provoking Reflection will oblige Your GRACE to vindicate Your own juſt Right, and the Crown's undoubted Prerogative.

If the Concern which I have in this Cauſe were the only thing in Queſtion, I ſhould make a Conſcience of giving Your GRACE any Trouble about it. But, my LORD, 'tis a Cauſe of far more extenſive and more important Conſequence. 'Tis the noble Cauſe of Your Country, in which Your GRACE has been ſo Active and ſo Succeſsful, and in which this Play was alter'd ; 'tis the Cauſe of Dramatick Poetry, the Cauſe of the *Britiſh* Muſes, and of all thoſe whom They vouchſafe to inſpire. 'Tis Your GRACE who is to determine whether theſe ſhall Flouriſh for the future, and do Honour to *Great Britain,* and conſequently to augment, in ſome meaſure,

the

DEDICATION.

the Interest and Power of Your Country; or whether the best Professors of the noblest Art, and the Art it self, must die. 'Tis Your GRACE who is to determine, whether Gentlemen who have great Capacities, who have had the most generous Education, who have all their Lives had the best and the noblest Designs for the Service of their Country, and the Instruction of Mankind, shall have their worthy Labours supported and render'd effectual to the great Ends for which they intended them; or whether they must all be sacrific'd to two or three Insolent Actors, who have no Capacity, who have had no Education, who have not the least Concern for their Country, who have nothing in their Heads or in their Hearts but low Thoughts, and sordid Designs; and yet at the same time have so much Pride, and so much insupportable Insolence, as to dare to fly in the Face of the greatest Persons in *England*.

I will now lay the Matter of Fact before Your GRACE, by which I believe you will very easily Discern, that there was a Conspiracy from the beginning, between the three Members of this separate Ministry, as they are pleas'd to call themselves, for the Destruction of this Play. They were engaged to Act it the last Winter by their Words solemnly given, and the acting of it then had been most seasonable, when the Nation was in the uneasy Expectation of a Double Invasion from *Sweden* on the *North*, and from *Spain* on the *West* of *England*. Instead of keeping their Words with me; they Postpon'd a Play, that was writ in the Cause of their Country, in the Cause of their Sovereign,

whose

DEDICATION.

whose Servants as well as Subjects they call themselves, for the most Absurd and Insipid Trifles that ever came upon any Stage. They began the Winter with preaching up Adultery to the Town by the Mouth of a Dramatick Priest: They ended it much after the rate at which they began it, by teaching Ladies how they may Cuckold their Husbands without the Apprehension of a Discovery; as if any License, or any Patent, would bear these People out in Debauching the People, or as if such a Practice were not sufficient to disannul any Patent. My LORD, in the beginning of this Winter they began to rehearse the Play, after they had dispos'd some of the Comick Parts to Persons who were wholly unfit for them; and maim'd two of the principal Tragick Scenes to that Degree, that I could hardly know them. After about five Weeks Rehearsal, the tenth of *November* was fix'd for the Acting the Play. I could not prevail with them to put it off for a Week longer, notwithstanding it was most apparently their Interest more than mine; because there was a daily Expectation of the KING's Arrival. My LORD, when the Tenth of *November* came, these three Religious Persons were, to the wonder of all that heard of it, attack'd with Scruples of Conscience: They were inform'd that it was the Third Day of a Young Author at the other House; and it would be Cruel, it would be Barbarous to have my First Day upon the other's Third. Thus did these good-natur'd Gentlemen take an occasion from a pretended Tenderness to exercise a real Barbarity. My LORD, I was very easily prevail'd

DEDICATION.

vail'd with to put off the Play; but little thought, at the same time, that they defign'd to put it off for a Day only. I was very much furpriz'd when I found by the Bills, that the Play was to be Acted the very next Day, and that confequently *Friday* was to be my Third Day: Now, My L o r d, *Friday* is not only the very worft Day of the Week for an Audience, but this was that particular *Friday*, when a Hundred Perfons who defign'd to be there, were either gone to meet the KING, or preparing here in Town to do that Duty, which was expected from them at His Arrival.

Thus, My L o r d, did thefe good, human, tender-hearted Managers take an occafion to exercife a real Barbarity upon their old Acquaintance, to whom they and their Stage are more oblig'd than to any Writer in *England*, from a pretended Tendernefs to one who is a meer Stranger to them, and from whofe Succefs they could expect nothing but the leffening of their Gain. My L o r d, the Play was Acted on *Wednefday* the 11th to an Audience of near a Hundred Pound, for fo much they own'd to me. It was favourably received by the Audience. There did fome Malice appear twice, but it was immediately drown'd by the utmoft Clamours of Applaufe. On *Thurfday* the Play was Acted again to an Audience of between Fifty and Threefcore Pounds. And on *Friday* to an Audience of between Sixty and Seventy Pounds. Confidering the Difadvantages under which we lay, here were fair hopes for the future. And on *Friday*, after the Play was done, thefe tender-hearted Managers caus'd another to be given out, to the Aftonifhment of

A 4
the

DEDICATION.

the Audience, the Disappointment of those who had reserv'd themselves for the Sixth Day, and the Retrenching three parts in four of my Profits; and this contrary to an Ancient Rule, which has been always observ'd till now by those who have at any time had the Government of a Playhouse, and that is, never to give over a new Play which is favourably received by an Audience as long as it brings Charges. And, My Lord, nothing can be more reasonable and equitable than the Observation of this Rule. For since the Poet ventures his Interest in his Play, which is sometimes his All, and his Reputation into the bargan, which is his Hope of future Gain, can any thing be more Just, than that the Masters or Managers of a Play-house should venture their Gain upon a probable prospect of future Profit, the loss of which for two or three Nights they will hardly feel, rather than by laying down a Play abruptly, absolutely ruin the Author, who perhaps has done his part to please.

Now, my Lord, I appeal to Your Grace, if here was not a fair Prospect of Success for the future: The Play had been acted three Nights together, to a Hundred, to Sixty, and to Seventy Pound. The Play was receiv'd the first Night with Applause: The KING, and the Court, and the Parliament, were all coming to Town. But notwithstanding all our reasonable Expectation, the Managers gave out another Play, insolently declaring, that no Play was worth their Acting any longer than it brings a Hundred Pound. Now, my Lord, they cannot but know that several Plays which have been but indifferently follow'd the first Days, have after-

wards

DEDICATION.

wards come to be admir'd Plays, and to bring crowded Audiences. The beſt Play which can be writ by an Author who has not a Cabal, will hardly bring a Hundred Pound upon the ſecond and fourth Nights; and the worſt that can be writ by a Poetaſter who has a Cabal, may do a great deal more. As long as the publick Taſte is ſo vitiated as it is at preſent, bad Plays are like to be more crowded than good ones. So that, by their own Declaration, as long as theſe Perſons have the Management of the Play-houſe, there can be no Improvement of the publick Taſte; good Writers are ſure to be diſcourag'd, and the Art of the Drama, in a little time, is certain to be loſt; and the Art of Writing is ſure to be followed by the Art of Acting. For great Actors are not to be made but by Original Parts; and as 'tis an eternal general Rule, that a Copy has neither the free Spirit nor eaſy Grace of an Original, ſo the Copy of a Copy is ſtill more faint, and the ſeveral ſucceeding Copies grow weaker ſtill the further they deſcend from the Original, till all Life and all Reſemblance comes at laſt to be loſt. But if any one happens to ob-ject to him, that when a young Man who has a Talent for Acting comes to Act a Part of which he has ſeen neither the Copying nor Original Actor, that Part is to him an Original one. To him I anſwer, that moſt of our Poets having had either the Addreſs or the Weakneſs, I leave it to Your GRACE to determine which, to write to the Manners and the Talents of ſome parti-cular Actors, it ſeems to me to be abſolutely im-poſſible, with Submiſſion to Your GRACE's Judgment, that any Actor can become an ad-mirable Original, by Playing a Part which was

writ

DEDICATION.

writ and defign'd for another Man's particular
Talent.

Thus have I laid before Your GRACE the
Reasons why the Conduct of the present Managers must destroy the very Species of Dramatick
Poets and Players. And these Reasons, which
I hope are clear in themselves, are confirm'd by
infallible Experience: It being evident from Fact,
that all our principal Dramatick Poets and Players have been form'd while our Theatres were
under the Lord Chamberlain's Regulation ; and
that both Writing and Acting have gradually
fall'n off, since the Players have pretended to
exclude him from his Jurisdiction over them.
And, my LORD, 'tis a melancholy thing to con-
sider, that there is not at present in *Great Britain* one promising Genius, or promising Actor,
growing up for the Stage.

As every Branch of Poetry in *England* must
fall with the Dramatick, there being here no
constant visible Encouragement for Poets, but
what is deriv'd from the Stage, I appeal to
Your GRACE, whether it is worth while, to
turn Poetry, which is the noblest, and perhaps
the only Original Branch of the *British* Learn-
ing, out of the Nation, only to advance the
Lucre of three Actors.

Thus, My LORD, have I laid this Cause before Your GRACE ; not without flattering my
self, that I have fully made it appear to You,
that I have been us'd with extream Injustice
by the Managers of the Play-house. Before
this Play came upon the Stage, it had the Ap-
probation of some of the very best Judges in
England, who are so, and are universally ac-
knowledg'd to be so, and who are too exal-
ted

DEDICATION.

ted both by their High Stations, and the Greatneſs of their Minds, to ſay a thing to me, which they did not think. I have had this Play long enough by me to form as true and as ſure a Judgment of it my ſelf, as any one can do, who underſtands Poetical Matters no better than my ſelf. And as a Man who is oppreſt is allow'd to ſpeak Truth in his own behalf, I humbly conceive, that nothing comparably to it has been produced at the Theatre in *Drury-Lane*, ſince theſe People had the Management of it, not excepting Mr. *Cibber*'s *Heroick Daughter*, who, for ought I know, may be more Heroick than the Daughter of *Corneille*; but there is this remarkable Difference between them, that *Corneille*'s is Beautiful and Spiritual, and Mr. *Cibber*'s Ugly and Inſipid.

My LORD, I humbly beg Your GRACE'S Pardon, for ſpeaking theſe few Words in my own behalf, which I do not abſolutely deſpair of obtaining, when I conſider that *Cibber* has lately employed thirty Pages in his own fulſom Commendation.

My LORD, the Mention of this Player naturally brings me to another thing which Your GRACE is now to determine; and that is, whether this is not only mine, but the Cauſe of Dramatick Poetry it ſelf, of all the Writers, and of all the Lovers of it: I hope I have made it appear, that all theſe join with me in this Petition to Your GRACE for a Redreſs of intollerable Grievances, which none but the KING and Your GRACE can Redreſs; that we who have ſcorn'd to be Slaves to our Princes, may be no longer ſubject to the ridiculous Tyranny of our

own

DEDICATION.

own wretched Creatures, our own Tools and Inftruments; that They may no longer fet up for Judges in their own Caufe, which *Englifhmen* would never allow to their Kings; that They may no longer ufurp a Government, which they have neither Capacity, nor Equity, nor Authority to fupport, and of which Your GRACE is the Lawful Monarch. How glorious will it be for Your GRACE to Protect and Preferve fo noble an Art, and the only reafonable publick Diverfion that ever was yet invented! And how much will it endear Your GRACE's Name and Memory to all the Writers and Lovers of Dramatick Poetry, both prefent and to come! My LORD, as all thofe Perfons will be highly pleafed with an Alteration in the Management of the Stage, they certainly expect it from Your GRACE's Beneficence, from Your Love to Your Country, from Your Knowledge and Love of Letters, and from the Greatnefs of Your Mind. I am,

My LORD,

Your GRACE's

moft Obedient, and

moft Humble Servant,

John Dennis.

PROLOGUE,

Spoken by Mr. *MILLS.*

THE *Tragedy we represent to Day*
Is but a Grafting upon Shakespear's *Play,*
In whose Original we may descry,
Where Master-strokes in wild Confusion lye,
Here brought to as much Order as we can
Reduce those Beauties upon Shakespear's *Plan;*
And from his Plan we dar'd not to depart,
Least Nature should be lost in Quest of Art :
And Art had been attain'd with too much Cost,
Had Shakespear's *Beauties in the Search been lost.*
As Philomel, *whom Heav'n and* Phœbus *teach,*
Has Notes which Birds, that Man instructs, ne'er reach.
" *So* Shakespear, *Fancy's sweetest Child,*
" *Warbles his Native Wood-Notes wild.*   Milton.
While ev'ry Note takes the rapt Heroe's Heart,
And ev'ry Note's victorious over Art.
Then what is ours, to Night, excuse for Shakespear's *Part.*
You chiefly, who are truly Britons *nam'd,*
Whose Breasts are with your Country's Love inflam'd,
Whose martial Toils as long as Time shall live,
Whose Conquests Credit to old Fables give :
Conquests which more renown'd by Age shall grow,
To which ev'n late Posterity shall owe
The noblest History the World can show;
You in our just Defence must sure engage,
And shield us from the Storms of Factious Rage.
In the same Cause in which each Champion fights,
In the same noble Cause our daring Poet writes.
For as when Britain's *Rebel Sons of late*
Combin'd with Foreign Foes t'invade the State,
She to your Valour and your Conduct owes,
That she subdued and crush'd her num'rous Foes :
We shew, to Night, such Treasons to prevent,
That their Guilt's follow'd by their Punishment,
That Heav'n's the Guardian of our Rightful Cause,
And watches o'er our Sov'reign and our Laws.

EPILOGUE

EPILOGUE,

Written by the Author, and intended to be Spoken.

NOW, Sirs, we wait to know if the same Doom
    Attends our Heroe here that did at Rome.
By Noise and Uproar he was driven from thence,
While Merit was a poor and weak Defence:
But let him not by those be banish'd hence.
If he was banish'd thence, 'twas against Right,
And done by the mad Rabble's beastly Spight;
If the same Spight his Merit here attends,
Perhaps too here he'll find the chosen few his Friends.
But if these Friends prove weak in his Defence,
And he and Shakespear must be driven hence;
As when he formerly was banish'd Rome,
He led the Volscians on to urge its Doom;
So now he Swears, in his impetuous Rage,
Jack-Puddings, Eunuchs, Tumblers shall engage,
To damn the Muses, and destroy the Stage.

ADVERTISEMENT.

THE Epilogue which follows was writ by Mr. *Cibber*, and spoke by Mrs. *Oldfield*. I never could get a sight of it before it was spoke, and when it was spoke, I heard it at such a distance from Mrs. *Oldfield*, that I heard it very imperfectly. When I came to read it, I found it to be a wretched Medley of Impudence and Nonsense. As I saw he had made exceeding bold with me, so I found, that like a very honest Gentleman, he had betray'd the Trust repos'd in him, and endeavour'd to give the Audience an ill Impression of the Play. At the latter end of the Epilogue, there is an appearance of Loyalty, which sav'd the whole from the Fate which had otherwise attended it. But 'tis as easy for Mr. *Cibber* at this time of Day to make a Bounce with his Loyalty, as 'tis for a Bully at Sea, who had lain hid in the Hold all the time of the Fight, to come up and swagger upon the Deck after the Danger is over. I would fain hear of some Proof that he gave of his Zeal for the Protestant Succession, before the King's Accession to the Crown, or some Proof which he has given since by any Action which was not to get him Money, and bring the Court to his Play. I am perfectly satisfied that any Author who brings a Play to *Drury-Lane*, must, if 'tis a good one, be sacrificed to the Jealousie of this fine Writer, unless he has either a powerful Cabal, or unless he will flatter Mr. *Robert Wilks*, and make him believe that he is an excellent Tragedian; which would be as Ridiculous and as absurd, as it would be to Compliment a Fellow in a Fair upon his walking on the High Rope, who is only a Tumbler; or as it would be to compliment Mr. *Cibber* upon his Masterpieces in Tragedies, *Perolla*, and the *Heroick Daughter*, which are as full of Nonsense and False *English* even as this Epilogue, and are full of stiff, awkward, affected Stuff, and Lines that make as hideous a Noise, as if they were compos'd in an Itinerant Wheel-Barrow.

    To end as I began with the Epilogue; if any Reader can tell me the meaning of some Lines in it, *erit mihi magnus Apollo.* EPI-

EPILOGUE, Written by Mr. *CIBBER*,
Spoken by Mrs. *OLDFIELD*.

OF late, moſt Authors, when their Plays are done,
   Contrive to ſend us prating Women on;
As if our Wiſe Haranguing could not fail
T' appeaſe the Critick, as when under Sail
Ships throw an empty Barrel to a Whale.
But hold————don't thus Affront us?————
That Criticks are like Whales, ſo far's but Civil,
But that a Woman is a Barrel————O! the Devil!
O ho! Now at his ſenſeleſs Wit I partly gueſs!
Barrels, he thinks, may well our Forms expreſs;
He means, we're like for Sound, and Hoops, and Hollowneſs:
Sweetly concluding it of courſe muſt follow,
The Part of Woman moſt deſir'd, her Heart, is hollow.
And pray, what's Man then, to return his Jeſt?
Why, when a Woman's well provok'd, a Beaſt;
For on their wiſeſt Heads, we can clap Horns at leaſt.
Barrels! A ſawcy Puppy! ſenſeleſs Rogue!
'Gad, I've a mind to Damn his Epilogue!
His Play I need not————no; poor wretched Elf!
That Matter's Rug! He's done that Jobb himſelf.
He has preacht Morals to wild Engliſh Brains,
In ſtupid Hopes, you'll thank him for his Pains.
Whoe'er from Tragick Scenes Succeſs would ſee,
Should give your various Taſtes Variety;
Inſtead of Camps and War, Lovers, and Grotts,
To ſwell the Fair with Sighs and———— pretty Thoughts,
(Tho' Criticks muſt be pleas'd,) h'as feaſted them with Faults,
Or that his Fancy might no Taſte eſcape,
Have treated Rakes of Pleaſure with a Rape;
Or, to ſecure him Friends, ſhewn other Sights;
For Whiggs, aſſerted Liberty, and Rights;
Or a Deſpotick King ——— for Jacobites.
And then, when things were brought to th' laſt Confuſion,
Have ſhewn, what honeſt Men might make their Uſe on,
What here, all Parties join'd in once ——— a Revolution.
Tcis could not fail————Nay, ſome ſtill keep ſuch Pother,
They lik'd the One ſo well, they want Another!
Why here, for half a Crown, you might have ſeen
What Madneſs 'twere to live ſuch Days again.
Had he ſhewn Laws infring'd, or let you ſee
The Sweets of Rectilineal Tyranny,
Or laſht thoſe Wretches, who, while free, complain
They're robb'd of their Hereditary Chain,
And Fine for Kings ——— fit only on the Stage to Reign,
You that adore 'em then might here enjoy 'em,
Whilſt Men with Hearts, like Beaſts of Prey annoy 'em:
To ſhut them hence, let Free-born Souls endeavour
That BRUNSWICK's Line may give us KINGS for Ever.

Dramatis Personæ.

MEN.

Caius Martius Coriolanus,		Mr. *Booth.*
Aufidius,		Mr. *Mills.*
Menenius,		Mr. *Corey.*
Cominius,		Mr. *Thurmond.*
Sicinius,	Two Tribunes	Mr. *W. Wilks.*
Brutus,	of the People.	Mr. *Walker.*
Lucius Cluentius,		Mr. *Boman,* Sen.
Titus Largius,		Mr. *Williams.*
Ædile,		Mr. *Oates.*
1ſt Citizen,		Mr. *Bickerſtaff.*
2d Citizen	Of *Coriolanus*'s	Mr. *Penkethman.*
3d Citizen,	Party.	Mr. *Johnſon.*
4th Citizen,		Mr. *Miller.*
1ſt Citizen,	Of *Sempronius*'s	Mr. *Norris.*
2d Citizen,	Party.	Mr. *Croſs.*
1ſt Servant,		Mr. *Penkethman.*
2d Servant,	To *Aufidius,*	Mr. *Norris.*
3d Servant,		Mr. *Miller.*

WOMEN.

Volumnia, Mother to *Coriolanus,*	Mrs. *Porter.*
Virgilia, Wife to *Coriolanus,*	Mrs. *Thurmond.*

Senators of *Rome,* and *Antium;* Citizens, Soldiers,
Ladies and Attendants.

The SCENE *is partly in* Rome, *and partly
in the Territories of the* Volſcians.

THE

THE

INVADER of his Country:

OR,

The FATAL RESENTMENT.

ACT I. SCENE I.

An Alarm; and after it enter Cominius *and three Tribunes of the Legions.*

COMINIUS.

ALT! give the Word.
   1 *Trib.* Halt!
   2 *Trib.* Halt!
   3 *Trib.* At length they make a Stand.
   Com. Lightning confound them! had
      they shewn in Battel
But half the Fury of this headlong Flight,
The Victory had past Dispute been ours.
With what resistless Eagerness they ran,
And with what Slaughter curs'd *Aufidius* follow'd!
Who now stands low'ring upon yonder Brow,
And threatens, like a Storm, to pour upon us.

B

What

What Force, what Spirit have we to receive him?
O Death to all my Hope of Fame and Conquest!
We shall be routed shamefully, entirely:
Rome for two hundred Years has been victorious,
And never lost a Battel till this Hour.
O cruel Gods! that thus have chose *Cominius*
To give th' Example of ignoble Flight.

   1 *Trib.* My Lord, one Comfort is remaining yet;
Methought that in the Intervals of Fight,
I now and then distinctly heard th' Assaults
Of those our Friends that lye before *Corioli.*

   2 *Trib.* I heard them plainly, and their shouts of
      Triumph,
Which Southern Gusts convey'd and snatch'd by turns
     from us.

   Com. Ye Gods, who have determin'd *Rome* shall rise
By War, to be the Mistress of the Universe,
O give them sudden Victory, and bring them
With all their Forces, and their Heroe *Marcius,*
To turn the Fortune of the Field and *Rome.*

   1 *Trib.* Who comes there?
   2 *Trib.* Stand!
   3 *Trib.* Give the word!
          Enter Lucius Cluentius.

   L. Cluent. Mars and *Quirinus!*
   1 *Trib. Lucius Cluentius* from *Corioli.*
   Com. Tribune, thy News! what Fortune have our
      Friends?
How fares the Hope of *Rome,* the noble *Marcius?*
   1 *Trib.* Well, as I hope, but that the Gods best know.
   Com. Ha! What dost thou mean?
Answer, in what condition didst thou leave him?
   L. Cluent. Cover'd with Fame, and crown'd with
      Victory,
And warmly he pursu'd the flying *Volscians.*
   Com. Thou mistak'st:
The *Volscians,* to which *Marcius* stands oppos'd
With *Titus Largius,* are within *Corioli.*

                  L. Cluent.

L. Cluent. Yes, but this Morning, at the break of Day,
With all their Force they made a desperate Sally,
And beat our bravest *Romans* to their Trenches:
Till rallied and led up by noble *Marcius,*
They seem'd to take new Life, new Fire from Him,
And breath'd, and look'd, and fought once more like
   Romans.
Then we turn'd Chasers who before were hunted,
And quickly made the *Volscians* seek for Shelter
Amidst their Wives and Children.

   Com. O would to all the Gods that thou wouldst end
As nobly thou begin'st!

   L. Cluent. Marcius, still foremost in the chase of Glory,
Hung like Destruction on their broken Rear,
And made a dreadful Slaughter of their Flyers;
Up to their Gates, expanded to receive them,
Swift as consuming Lightning he pursu'd them,
Still blasting, as he follow'd; when, curs'd Moment!—

   Com. And fatal Pause! Go on, for I'm prepar'd
To hear the worst of Fate.

   L. Cluent. O wonderful, but oh disastrous Valour!
Marcius, transported by his matchless Fire,
Enters the Town impetuous with the *Volscians;*
And while our fiercest *Romans* stopt and paus'd,
Struck and astonish'd at the wond'rous Action,
With Horror and Confusion I beheld
The massy Gates returning on their Hinges,
And *Marcius* shut among ten thousand Foes,
And left alone expos'd to all their Fury.

   Com. O noble *Roman!*
Marcius is slain, the Hope of *Rome* is gone;
For thou wouldst die, I know, a thousand Deaths,
Before thou wouldst be Captive to the *Volscians.*
Tho' thou speak'st Truth, methinks thou speak'st not
How long is't since this fatal Action happen'd? [well.

   L. Cluent. Above an Hour, my Lord.

   Com. Corioli is distant but a Mile,
And hither we distinctly heard their Drums;

How

How couldst thou in a Mile confound an Hour,
And bring thy News so late?

   L. Cluent. Spies of the *Volsci*
Held me in chase, that I was forc'd to wheele
Three or four Miles about; or else, my Lord,
I had in less than half the time been here.

   Com. Hie thee to *Rome*, and let the Senate know this;
And tell them I my self have been repuls'd,
And that each moment I'm in expectation
Of being once more attack'd by fierce *Aufidius.*

                        [Exit Cluent.

Enter a fourth Tribune.

   4 *Trib.* My Lord, *Aufidius* leads his *Volscians* down
Into the Plain, and seems resolv'd t' attack us.

   Com. Are all the Soldiers ready to receive them?

   4 *Trib.* Their Hands are ready, but their Hearts are

   Com. Then all, I fear, is lost.   [weak.
Farewel, O *Rome*, and thou, O Life, farewel!
For I will ne'er return Inglorious home;
And know, O *Rome*, that he who for thee Dies,
Does more than he who Conquers. Ha! who's yonder,
That looks as he were flea'd all o'er? O Gods!
That Figure and that Stamp I've seen before,
And nobly painted thus with Hostile Blood.
'Tis sure the Ghost of *Marcius* come from Hell,
To be reveng'd of the perfidious *Volscians.*

   Marc. [*Within.*] Come I too late?

   Com. By Immortal *Jove* 'tis he! he lives, he lives:
The Shepherd knows not Thunder from a Tabor,
More than I know the Sound of *Marcius*' Voice,
From every meaner Man's.

Enter Marcius.

   Marc. Come I too late?

   Com. Yes, if you come not in the Blood of others,
But mantled in your own.

   Marc. Oh let me clasp thee!
In Arms as sound as when I woo'd, in Heart
Jocund as when our Nuptial Day was done,
And Tapers burnt to Bedward.

                           Com.

Com. What Wonder, or what God has brought thee hither?

Lucius Cluentius brought the fatal News
But now, that thou wert shut within *Corioli.*

Marc. You heard the Truth.

Com. What God, propitious to the Fate of *Rome,*
Wrought thy Deliverance so very soon,
So very unexpectedly?

Marc. I want both Time and Breath t'inform you now.

Com. Thou Flower of Warriors, how fares *Titus
Largius?*

Marc. As the Man fares who does the work of Fate,
Condemning some to Death, and some to Exile;
Ransoming some, some pitying, threatning others:
Holding *Corioli* in the Name of *Rome,*
E'en like a fawning Greyhound in the Leash,
To let them slip at pleasure.
But see he comes himself t'inform you further.

Enter Largius.

Com. More Wonders! welcome, *Titus;* thou art come
Most unexpected, in a lucky Hour.

Larg. Oh General! see there the noble Steed,
For we are but the bare Caparison.
Oh I have Miracles to entertain thee,
Transcending all Belief, surpassing all Example.
Behold that Wonderful, that Godlike Man,
Who when he was enclos'd among ten thousand,
Drove them, like some Divinity, before him;
Infusing mortal Terrors thro' their Souls:
Then to our *Romans* open'd wide their Gates,
And let in mighty Ruin on them all.

Com. Thou Heroe of the Age, and God of War,
With Wonder I survey thee.

Marc. No more, I do beseech you.
My Mother has a Right t'extoll her Blood;
Yet when she praises me, she always grieves me:
This is a time for Action, not for Talk.
Hast thou brought any Succours to us, *Titus?*

B 3 *Larg.*

Larg. All but a few who stay to guard the Town,
For one short Hour or two.
For if we win the Field, the Town is ours;
But losing that, we lose of course the other.

Marci. Where lies the Enemy? Are we Lords of the
If not, why, General, cease we till we are so?   [Field?

Com. *Marcius,* we have to disadvantage fought,
And now expect to be attack'd again.

Marci. The Men half vanquish'd are, who are attack'd;
Let us march up to them without delay,
And be ourselves th' Attackers.
How lies their Battle? Know you on what Side
They have plac'd their Men of Trust?

Com. As near as I can guess, my Noble *Marcius,*
They who compose their Center are the *Veterans,*
On whom they most rely, commanded by
Tullus Aufidius, their successful General.

Marci. A fortunate and formidable Leader.
Were there a Man on Earth whom I cou'd envy,
It should be this *Aufidius;*
And were I any thing but what I am,
I then could wish that I were only he.

Com. You have fought together.   [other,

Marci. Were half this Globe in Conflict with the
And he upon my Party, I'd revolt
That I might combat him; he is a Lyon,
Whom I am proud to hunt; therefore beseech you,
By all the Battles we have fought together,
By all the Blood we have together shed,
And by the solemn Vows which we have made
To let no Time dissolve our bond of Friendship,
I beg you that you would directly set me
Against this fierce *Aufidius* and his *Antiats;*
And that without the least delay we march,
Filling the Air with Swords and Darts advanc'd,
And make ev'n this the great deciding Hour.

Com. Tho' I could wish
You were conducted to a gentle Bath,

And

And healing Balm infus'd into your Wounds,
Yet dare I ne'er deny what *Marcius* asks:
Then let the Soldiers strait surround this Tent,
And take your choice of those who are most fit,
To imitate thy great and bright Example.

Marci. They are most proper who are the most willing,
If there be such, which were a Crime to doubt;
Who love this noble Paint with which I'm dy'd;
If here are any who are less afraid
Of dangers to their Persons, than their Fames,
If any think brave Death outweighs bad Life,
And that his Country's dearer than himself,
Let all who find these noble Dispositions
Advance their Swords, to shew their Resolutions,
Such are my Friends, my Brethren and my Countrymen,
And only such are fit to follow *Marcius*.

[*They all shout and flourish their Swords.*

1st Sold. Lead on, brave *Marcius*, thee we follow all
To Death or Victory.

All. To Death or Victory we follow all.

Com. Was ever such a sudden wondrous Change?
They look, they move, they breath with other Souls,
And more than mortal Fury.   [*Shout again.*

Marci. Ay, in that Shout the *Volscian* Army fell;
Yes, my brave Friends, ye have already conquer'd,
I see it in your Eyes, I hear it in your Voices.
Come on, and I, as Time does Fate, will lead you
To Slaughter and unbounded Devastation.

All. To Death or Victory lead on, brave *Marcius.* [*Exe.*

[*Alarm as in Battle.*

Enter Marcius *and* Aufidius *at several Doors.*

Marci. I'll fight with none but thee, for I do hate thee
Worse than a Promise-breaker.

Auf. We hate alike.
Not *Africk* owns a Serpent I abhor
More than thy Fame and Envy; fix thy Foot.

Marci. Let the first Starter dye the other's Slave;
And after that most ignominious Death,

B 4   May

May the Gods doom him to eternal Torments.

Aufid. If I fly, *Marcius,* hoot me like a Hare.

Marci. Tullus Aufidius, know, within these three
Alone in your *Corioli* I fought,   [*Hours*
Alone in your *Corioli* I vanquish'd.
Where walking like the Substitute of *Jove,*
I with this single Arm dealt Fate amongst them.
Believ'st thou 'tis my Blood with which I'm mark'd?
No: 'tis thy dearest Friends, and thy Relations.
Now rouse thy Faculties to great Revenge,
And scrue them to the utmost height of Fury.

Aufid. Think'st thou, when I behold thy hated Face,
want to be provok'd by Words to kill thee?
Thou say'st, I see upon thy painted Skin
The Blood of my dear Friends, and my Relations:
Thou Fool, what's that to t'other stabbing Sight,
When in thy haughty and insulting Eyes
I see thy boasted Triumphs o'er *Aufidius.*
Yes, that's the Sight that works my Rage to Madness,
And in me kindles such a raging Feaver,
That if 'tis not extinguish'd by thy Blood
I'll quench it with my own.

Marci. Then take thy Wish,
Have at thy Life, and all the *Volscian* Pow'r.

> [*Here they fight, and certain* Volscians *come to the Aid of* Aufidius; Marcius *fights till they are driven in breathless.*

Auf. to his Men. Stand from between us, oh, stand
          off, I charge you.
Stand off, ye Scandals to the Fame of *Tullus!*
Base and officious Cowards, how did you dare
To think that I, engaged against one *Roman,*
Could stand in need of you?

> [*Flourish, Alarm. A Retreat is sounded.*
Enter at one Door Cominius *with the* Romans, *at another Door* Marcius. *The Soldiers proclaim the Victory of* Cominius.

Com. Enough, my kind Companions of the War,
                                              You

You force me to usurp another's Right,
For there's the Heroe to whom all is due:
'Tis he who sav'd your Persons, sav'd your Names,
And did immortal Honour to your Country;
Who rais'd *Cominius* to eternal Fame,
Ev'n from the brink of everlasting Infamy.
Oh *Caius*, *Caius*, I am lost in Wonder;
For I this Day have seen thee do such things,
Such more than mortal things, that should'st thou now
Hear with deliberate Calmness what before
Thou didst with godlike Fury, much I question
Whether thou wouldst not start at the Relation,
And doubt the Truth of thy own History.

Marci. Enough, enough, my General, and too much.
I have some Wounds upon me, and they smart
To hear themselves remember'd.

Com. But base Forgetfulness might make them angry,
And black Ingratitude might make them fester.
However, *Marcius*, so far thou art right,
That Talk is but a barren Recompence
For thy unequall'd Merit.
Therefore I'll say no more, 'till I report it
Where Senators shall mingle Tears with Smiles,
Where great *Patricians* that are used to Victory
Shall start, and shrug, and lift their Eyes to Heaven;
Where Matrons shall grow pale at the Relation,
Trembling with pleasure intermix'd with horrour;
Yet greedy still, devour the wondrous Tale:
Where the dull Tribunes, and the rank *Plebeians*,
That have so long malign'd thy growing Glory,
Shall say, against their Hearts, we thank the Gods,
Our *Rome* hath such a Soldier. Yet this Victory
Thou gain'dst, when thou wert wearied more than half
By conquering with thy single Arm *Corioli*.

Marci. Nay, General ——

Com. Proceed we now to something more than Talk.
Then be it known to all the World that *Marcius*
By Merit wears the Laurel of this Victory;

And

And for a lasting Token of this Conquest,
My Noble Steed known to the Camp I give him,
With all his rich Caparison; from hence,
For what he did within *Corioli,* call him,
With all the applause and clamour of the Host,
Caius Marcius Coriolanus.

   All. Caius Marcius Coriolanus, Hail!

   All. All hail, *Coriolanus!*

   Marci. I will go wash, and when my Face is fair,
You shall perceive whether I blush or not.

   Com. Besides, of all the Horses, all the Treasure,
Whereof we have taken store in Field and City,
We render you the Tenth, to be chose out
Before the common Distribution's made.

   Marci. I thank you, General : but of all your Gifts
Your Steed and Noble Sirname I accept,
Which setting my old Honours still before me,
Shall gloriously excite my Soul to new ones.
But absolutely I refuse the rest,
And stand upon my common part with those
Who have been bare Spectators of the Victory.

   Com. Now, my Companions of the War, prepare
To march our conquering Legions back to *Rome!*
You, *Caius Marcius,* must remain with me.

                [*Exeunt all but* Comin *and* Coriol.

   Com. Now we must back to *Rome, Coriolanus,*
Where all will now give way to Joy and Transport,
T' unruly Joy, and to tumultuous Transport,
And there will be nor time, nor place for Council;
A word then to thy darling Interest now :
When we're at *Rome,* I know th' assembled Senate
At my Proposal will design thee Consul,
Be not thou wanting to thy own advancement.

   Cor. And how should I be wanting?

   Com. 's, *Caius,* thou art Brave beyond Example,
Thy Soul's possest of ev'ry peaceful Virtue,
Temperate, chast, observant of the Laws,
With an Integrity like that of *Jove,*
Above the Pow'r of Fortune or of Fate;   Yet

Yet thy one Blemish will all this disgrace.

Cor. Name it, my Lord.

Com. Thou hast a Soul too haughty and severe
For one who lives in a Free State, a State
That's so much founded on Equality.
You have been too harsh, and have provok'd the People.

Cor. I hate the People.

Com. Then give me leave to tell you, you're ungrateful;
For to this very People, whom you hate,
You more than half your matchless Conquests owe,
And more than half your Glory.

Cor. Owe them to them!

Com. To them, by whose Assistance you have conquer'd,
And in the Camp you cherish and esteem them.

Cor. Because they pay a blind Obedience here,
And ne'er dispute the Will of their Superiors;
At *Rome* they insolently aim at Pow'r,
And to controul the Nobles and the Senate,
And therefore there I hate them.

Com. The Discipline of War requires unbounded Sway,
But Peace restrains aspiring Pow'r by Law:
And when at *Rome* the People curb the Senate,
'Tis when th' ambitious Race of our *Patricians*
Seem aiming at that Tyranny themselves,
For which they expell'd the proud and cruel *Tarquin*.
Cherish the People when at *Rome* henceforward,
As here on *Volscian* Land you fight for them.

Cor. Is it for them I fight? Is it for them
I lose my dearest Blood?

Com. Is it not in thy Country's Cause thou fight'st?

Cor. Most certainly.

Com. And are the Walls or Fields thy Country then?

Cor. No; the *Patricians*, and the noble Senate.

Com. A narrow Country, of a poor Extent,
Not the tenth part so large as was our *Rome*,
When 'twas first founded by our Martial *Romulus*.
Thy Country is the People.   [Nature.

Cor. When they're but nam'd, they shock my very
                                        Com.

Com. And doeſt thou think thy Nature different then
From that of this ſo deſpicable People?
Know, what they are thy Anceſtors have been,
And what thou art will their Deſcendans be.
Alas, we're all compounded of one Stuff:
The Gods, who made us, no ſuch difference ſee,
Between *Patricians* and th' ignoble Vulgar?
But hark! the Trumpet calls; we muſt to *Rome*;
And as we march, let's in our Minds revolve,
That this brave People, whom ſo much thou hat'ſt,
Are deſtin'd by the Gods to rule the Univerſe.
By them our *Rome* ſhall to the Stars ariſe:
Whom the Gods favour, let not Man deſpiſe.

The End of the Firſt *ACT.*

ACT

ACT II. SCENE I.

Enter Volumnia, *and* Virgilia.

Vol. FIE, my *Virgilia*, leave these doleful Mur-
   murs:
Dreams are but idle Vapours without Meaning.
 Virg. Ay, but for five succeſſive Nights this Viſion
At dead of Night has viſited my Slumbers;
For five succeſſive Nights I've ſeen my Lord
Supriz'd, ſurrounded, murder'd by the *Volſcians*.
 Vol. The meer Deluſions of your Melancholy.
But, after all, ſuppoſe Preſage divine
Did by theſe Viſions break your reſtleſs Slumbers,
Should they perſwade you to throw off the *Roman*,
And to appear dejected and deſponding!
This is juſt counter to the Gods Deſign;
Why ſhou'd at any time divine Prediction
Deſcend, t' inform us of our future Fate?
Is it, that by foreſeeing we can ſhun
Th' Eternal Dictates of Almighty Will?
Or, that the Powers take barbarous Delight,
To plague the Minds of miſerable Mortals,
By vain Fore-knowledge of avoidleſs Ills?
No ſure; 'tis that our Souls without ſurpriſe
May be prepared to meet the worſt of Fate,
That we ſecure may view its ghaſtfull'ſt Terrors,
Stem with undaunted Breaſts a Flood of Evils,
And may, in ſhort, behave our ſelves like *Romans*,
And like the darling Offspring of the Gods.
            Virg.

Virg. You are the awful Parent of my *Marcius*
Do you not love your Son ?

Vol. Yes, with a Love, as tender, and as true,
As softest Mothers love their darling Children :
For which of them can show a Son like *Marcius*
To justifie her Fondness ? Such a Son
As my luxuriant, wanton Fancy form'd,
Such as my boldest, warmest Wishes pray'd for ;
Exactly such a one the Gods have sent me.
Yet such a Child, and such an only Child,
So cherish'd, so belov'd, (for all true Love
Is always regulated by th' Advantage
Of the beloved Object, not its own ;)
E're yet the Down his tender Cheek adorn'd,
While Youthful Beauty drew all Eyes upon him,
When, tho' a King should beg a live-long Day,
Some Mothers would not part with him an Hour ;
I, knowing Indolent, Inglorious Men
To be but Pictures, the dead Furniture
Of Houses that are Noble, that 'tis Glory
That ends what we begin, and makes the Man ;
Convinc'd of this, to a cruel War I sent him,
Where he thro' Manly Dangers hunted Fame,
And Brow-bound with the Oak came back to *Rome.*
I tell thee, Daughter, my Heart sprung not more
When first I heard there was a Man-child born,
Than when my Boy first prov'd himself a Man.

Virg. But can you think of his untimely Death,
And not feel Horror at the dreadful Thought ?

Vol. No ; at that Thought great Nature takes th' A-
    larm ;
Yes, at that Thought, those very piercing Terrors,
Those shadd'wing Horrors, which torment your Breast,
Begin to swell and tyrannize in mine,
But strait with *Roman* Spirit I subdue them ;
And still remain the Mistress of my Soul.
My Comfort is, that if my *Marcius* dies,
The noble Services he does for *Rome,*

And

And his Eternal Fame, shall be my Offspring.

Virg. I have a doleful, and a boding Heart.

Vol. I an auspicious, and a sprightly one,
And rather think that mine's inspir'd from Heaven.
Methinks I hither hear your Husband's Drums:
I see, I see him pluck *Aufidius* down;
While all the routed *Volscians* fly amain,
As Hunters from the roaring Lion fly,
And leave their General to my *Marcius*' Rage.
And thus methinks I see him Stamp, and thus
I hear him to our *Romans* cry aloud,
Come on, ye Cowards; ye were got in Fear,
Tho' ye were born in *Rome* : his Bloody Brow
With Iron Hand then wiping, on he goes,
Like to a Harvest Man, that's task'd to mow
Or all, or lose his Hire.

Virg. His Bloody Brow! Oh Heavens!

Vol. Away, you Fool; it more becomes a Man,
Than gilded Trophies, and triumphant Chariots.
The Breasts of *Hecuba* appear'd not lovelier,
When in her charming Bloom she suckled *Hector*;
Than *Hector*'s Forehead, when it spouted Blood,
In the contention against stern *Achilles*.

Virg. Heav'n guard my Lord from fell *Aufidius'*
Rage.

Vol. He'll beat *Aufidius'* Head below his Heel,
And tread upon his Neck. Alas, *Virgilia*!
What makes the Blood come mantling o'er thy Face,
And then departing leave a Death-like Pale?
Why is thy Eye thus fix'd? What mean these Starts,
And these convulsive Tremblings?

Virg. 'Tis he himself! it can be none but he.
That Godlike Form belongs to none but *Marcius*.
Protect me, and support me, all ye Powers.

     Enter Cominius, Coriolanus, *and* Menenius.

Cor. The Powers make me their Substitute for that;
'Tis I'll protect thee, and support thee now.
Come to my Heart, to which thou art more dear,
                     Than

Than the Life-Blood that warms it.

[*Cominius entertains* Volumnia.

Virg. Excess of Bliss, which I can never bear;
The mighty Joy, so sudden, so impetuous,
Consumes my Spirits, and devours my Life.
What Power has given thee to my eager Arms?
What God has snatcht thee from the Jaws of Fate;
And hither sent thee on the Wings of Love,
To stop my Hand, and cheer my dying Eyes?

Cor. The God of War, the God of Victory,
At the request of Love's propitious Goddess.

Virg. Of Victory? This is too much, ye Gods!
O fierce Convulsions of transporting Joy!
But see, the noblest Mother of the World
Remains too long neglected.

Cor. I knew not till this Moment she was here,
So much my Eyes and every busy Power
Of my rapt Soul were taken up with thee.

Vol. [*to Com.*] Now pour ten Thousand Blessings
    on him, Gods!
These are unparallel'd, unheard-of Wonders?

Com. This is not half the Truth.

Men. Conquest and Glory evermore like this.
Attend the Godlike Man!

Vol. O Joy, that lifts *Volumnia* to the Skies,
And places her among the deathless Gods!

Cor. Pardon, that I've so long delay'd my Knee;
For you, I know, have knelt to all the Gods
For my Prosperity.   [*Kneels.*

Vol. O *Marcius, Marcius,* O my Son, my Son,
Thou wondrous Prop of a declining State,
Support of *Rome,* and Glory of thy Race!
Thy joyful Mother's Ornament and Honour,
My worthy *Marcius,* my *Coriolanus!*
O rise, thou Turner of Despair to Victory,
Rise, thou sole glorious Conqueror of *Corioli.*

Cor. What, my Friend too? My good *Menenius*
here?

Men.

Men. Now the Gods crown thee!
'Tis Forty Years since last my Eyes were moist,
But all my Mother comes into them now:
Now welcome, welcome, yes, ten thousand Welcomes!
A Curse begin ev'n at his very Heart,
Who is not glad to see thee.

     Enter Messenger.

 Mess. My Lord, your Colleague and th' assembled
 Senate
Desire your Presence.

 Com. I come;
And, *Marcius*, you without delay must follow.

 Cor. I will.   [*Exit* Comin.

 Volum. Now all that ever my luxuriant Fancy
Invented, to indulge my fondest Wishes,
Is truly come to pass; there wants but one thing;
You must be Consul now, *Coriolanus.*

 Cor. Yes, if I can be so, without becoming
The Creature of the despicable Rabble.

 Men. Come to the Capitol; you are expected.

     [*Exeunt* Coriol. *and* Men.

 Vol. Now where's the dreadful Vision of the Night?
Marcius has been surrounded by the *Volscians*;
But singly, solely has o'ercome them all.
He with his single Arm subdu'd *Corioli*;
Then swift as Lightning joyn'd our routed Army:
And rallied them to Conquest and to Glory.
He was the very Soul of their vast Body,
Was all in all, and all in ev'ry part;
Where-e'er he went, before him Fortune flew,
And certain Fate attended on his March,
And Victory upon his dreadful Plume
Sate perch'd, and clapt her joyful Eagle's Wings:
Three times our *Marcius* singled out *Aufidius*,
And thrice the *Volscian* sunk beneath his Thunder,
And bent his Knee, as 'twere in Adoration

 Virg. Ye Gods!
These are transporting, and amazing things!

     C   *Volum.*

Volum. Hark! how the People ſhout! Come, let's
    go gaze
Upon his unpremeditated Triumph.   [*Ex.*

SCENE II.   *The Capitol.*

Enter Sicinius, *and* Brutus, *two Tribunes of the People.*

Brut. 'Tis true. the Death of *Tarquin* gave a looſe
To this outragious Pride of the *Patricians,*
Which till that Hour had been reſtrain'd thro' Fear;
Leſt the vex'd People ſhould recall their Monarch,
And rather chuſe one Tyrant than Three hundred.

Sicin. And yet this *Marcius,* now *Coriolanus,*
In Pride and Inſolence out-does them all.

Brut. When we were choſen Tribunes, you remem-
    ber
His Oppoſition, and his proud Deportment;
And when the People pin'd in the late Dearth,
'Twas he withſtood the giving them Relief,
By dealing them Corn *gratis.*

Sicin. His new Exploits will ſcarce abate his Pride,
Nor his new lofty Title.

Brut. No, nor this mad Reception of the People.
How in tumultuous Crowds they throng to ſee him,
And view their deadlieſt Foe with Lovers Eyes!
Blear'd Sights are ſpectacled to ſee him paſs,
And halting Crutches learn Activity;
And crying Babes into Convulſions fall,
While prattling Nurſes chat of none but him:
The Kitchin Malkin pinns her richeſt Buckram
About her reachy Neck, and up ſhe climbs,
And clings like Ivy to the Walls, to eye him.
Stalls, Windows, Bulks are ſmother'd up and choak'd,
The Leads of Houſes fill'd, and Ridges hors'd
With variable Complexions, all agreeing

                             In.

In Earnestness to see him ; cloister'd *Flamens*,
That shun the Eyes of Men, and leave Society,
To be quite swallow'd up in Contemplation,
Now labouring cleave the waving Crowd, and puff
To win a vulgar Station; our veil'd Dames
Commit the War of white and fine Carnation
In their nice lovely Cheeks, to be devour'd
By *Phœbus'* burning Kisses; such a Rage,
And such an universal Eagerness,
As if that whatsoever God who leads him
Were slyly crept into his human Powers,
And gave him graceful Posture.

   Sic. The Senate is resolv'd to chuse him Consul.
   Brut. And the mad People will confirm that Choice.
   Sic. Then our Authority is at an end.
   Brut. And with it Liberty.
   Sic. Our Comfort is,
That he wants Temper to support these Honours ;
And all that Pride, with which he threats the State,
Will, like an Engine manag'd without Skill,
Recoil upon himself.

   Brut. That is indeed a comfort.
   Sic. And doubt not, but the giddy changing Vulgar,
Whose Rights are in our keeping, will forget,
With the least Cause, the Glare of these Atchievements ;
Which Cause that he will give, I no more doubt,
Than his Presumption and his Insolence.

   Brut. I heard him swear,
Were he to stand for Consul, never would he
Appear i'th' *Roman Forum*, ne'er put on,
The candid Vesture of Humility :
Nor shewing (as the manner is) his Wounds
To the vile People, beg their stinking Breaths.

   Sic. 'Tis right.
   Brut. It was his word.
Oh, he would miss it, rather than obtain it;
But by the Suit of the Nobility,
And of the Gentry to him.

         Sic.

Sic. And may his evil Genius prompt him still
To hold that Purpose, and to execute it.

Brut. You may depend upon it, that he will.

Sic. It shall be like our Wishes then, Destruction to
him.

Brut. He or our Office must find sure Destruction:
Therefore we must insinuate to the People,
With what malignant Hatred he has vex'd them;
That to his Power he would have made them Mules;
Silenc'd their Pleaders, overturn'd their Freedoms:
Contemning them as Animals, as Beasts,
Incapable of Human Thought or Action;
And to be us'd like Camels in the War,
Who have their Provender for bearing Burdens,
And Blows for sinking under them.

Shout. Enter Citizen.

What's the matter?

Cit. The conquering *Coriolanus* comes this way:
I have seen the Deaf Men throng to see him walk,
The Blind to hear him speak; Matrons flung Gloves,
Virgins their Handkerchiefs and Silken Scarfs
Upon him as he pass'd, the Nobles bended
As to *Jove*'s Statue, and the Commons made
A show'r and thunder with their Caps and Shouts,
Such as I never heard before.

Brut. The Senate is broke up; see, *Caius Marcius*,
And with him comes *Cominius*, and *Menenius*.
Let us begone.   [*Exeunt.*

Enter Coriolanus, Cominius, *and* Menenius.

Com. The Senate have with wonder heard thy Deeds,
And have with one consent, for thy great Services,
Resolv'd to make thee Consul.
Anon you must bespeak the Peoples Voice.

Cor. I do beseech you,
Let me o'erleap that Custom, for I cannot
Put on the Gown, stand naked, and entreat them,
For my Wounds sake, to give their Suffrages:
From this be pleas'd that I may be excepted.

Com.

Com. Know, Sir, the Peoples Voices are their Rights,
Nor will they bate one jot of Ceremony.

Men. He shall not put them to it.
Go, pray Sir, and adapt you to the Custom,
And take, as all your Predecessors have done,
The Honour with the Form.

Cor. It is a Part which I shall blush in acting;
And what might well be taken from the People.
To brag unto them, Thus I did, and thus;
Shew them th' unaking Scars which I shou'd hide,
As if I had receiv'd them for the Hire
Of their Breath only.

Men. Come, come, no more; you must resolve to
do it:
So to our Noble Consul we wish Joy,
And all access of Honour.   [*Exeunt.*

SCENE III. *The Roman Forum.*

Enter several of Coriolanus *his Party.*

1 *Cit.* Come, come, Is there no false Brother a-
mong us? Are you all resolv'd to vote for *Coriolanus*?

All. All, all.

2 *Cit.* If he does require our Voices, we ought not
to deny him.

3 *Cit.* We may, Sir, if we will.

4 *Cit.* We have a Power in our selves to do it; but
'tis a Power that we have no Power to do. For if
he shew us his Wounds, and tell us his Deeds, we are
to put our Tongues into these Wounds, and speak for
them. So if he tell us his noble Deeds, we are like-
wise to tell him our noble acceptance of them. Ingratitude is monstrous, and for the Multitude to be
ungrateful, were to make a Monster of the Multitude;

of

of the which we being Members, fhould bring our felves to be monftrous Members.

1 *Cit.* And to make us no better thought of, a little help will ferve: For when we ftood up about the Corn, he himfelf ftuck not to call us the many-headed Multitude.

3 *Cit.* We have been call'd fo by many, not that our Heads are fome Brown, fome Black, fome Auborn, and fome Bald, but that our Wits are fo diverfely colour'd.   And truly I think, that if all our Wits were to go out of one Skull, they would fly *Eaft*, *Weft*, *North*, and *South*, and to every part of the Compafs.

2 *Cit.* Think you fo? Which Way do you judge my Wit would fly?

3 *Cit.* Thy Wit will not fo foon out as another's, 'tis ftrongly wedg'd up in a Blockhead.   Yet if it were once out, it would neither fly, nor run, nor walk, no nor creep: It would directly tend to its center of Gravity, and fink plumb down, with as much alacrity as a Millftone.

Enter feveral of Sempronius *his Party.*

All Sem. A *Sempronius!* A *Sempronius!*

All Cor. A *Coriolanus!* A *Coriolanus!*

All Sem. No Purfe-proud *Patrician!* no Contemner of the People.

All Cor. No Cuckold-making *Patrician!* no Denier of his own Hand.

1 *Sem.* Why, who denied his own Hand?

2 *Cor.* Why *Sempronins*, *Sempronius*.

2 *Sem.* Why here's an impudent Slander, my Mafters, when all the World knows that he can neither write nor read; by the fame token that he and I had the fame Education.

2 *Cor.* A rare Fellow for a Conful truly!

[*All* Coriolanus's *Party laugh.*

2 *Sem.* Ay marry is he, and to be valued for his natural parts. His Father faw, that he had fuch prodigious parts, that it would be in vain to teach him any

any thing. He found he never would have occafion for any Man's Wit but his own; and fo, my Mafters, a *Sempronius,* a *Sempronius!*

1 *Cor.* No Box and Dice Man! No Hap-Hazarder!

[*All C. laugh and flout.*

Look you, Sirs, we will not chufe a Man for Conful, who will be fure to make Chance his Deputy-Governor. He who has ruin'd his own Eftate by Hazard, is hardly like to fecure ours by Conduct.   [*All C. laugh.*

And fo I fay no *Sempronius.*

2 *Semp.* No Subverter of the Peoples Liberties, no *Coriolanus.*

1 *Cor.* Yes, *Coriolanus* is like to fubvert our Liberties, becaufe he is the only Man who has kept out young *Tarquin*; and *Sempronius* is like to fecure thefe Liberties, becaufe he has been all along in a Plot for the bringing him in. And in what manner for the bringing him in? Why wielding in his unconditional Arm a Spunge inftead of a Scepter, with which, when the Boy is difpos'd to be frolickfome, he may run about in Moon-light and rub out Milk-fcores.

All Cor. Ha, ha, ha! Liberty and Property! Liberty and Property! no *Sempronius,* no Spunger.

1 *Semp.* Hark you me, *Sanga!* Here you bawl out Liberty and Property! You owe me fifty Sefterces.

1 *Cor.* Well, Sir! Well, Sir!

1 *Semp.* And if you don't either vote for *Sempronius,* or pay me immediately, I will forthwith take both your Chattels and your Carcafe into *Salva Cuftodia*; and there's Liberty and Property for you, you Dog.

All Semp. Ha, ha, ha.

All Cor. What, does he threaten? Knock him down! knock him down!

1 *Semp.* Nay then,---The Temples of our Gods, the Temples of our Gods are in danger!

All Semp. The Temples of our Gods, the Temples of our Gods are in danger!

1 *Cor.*

1 *Cor.* Very fine! This *Sempronius* is a blessed Person indeed! he Games, he Cheats, he Swears, he Drinks, he Drabs; and yet whenever this Scoundrel is out of Place, all things are upon the brink of Ruin forsooth, our Temples are about to be turn'd Topsy-turvy, and the Gods to stand upon their Heads; as if nothing but profligate Vice could be the firm Support of Religion, or that the Gods were too weak to defend themselves without such Bully Backs to their Seconds.

1 *Semp.* Religion is like to come into mighty Repute indeed, when Fellows are about to come into play, who are so proud and so sawcy that they scorn to pull off their Hats to the Gods.

1 *Cor.* You lie, you Rogue, you lie, there are no such coming into play. Our Gods are like to be finely help'd up, by *Sempronius*'s bringing young *Tarquin* in. *Sempronius* and he have been travelling, with a murrain to them; they have been in *Ægypt* together, and now we must exchange our own for *Ægyptian* Gods; *Apollo* must give Place to a Leek, *Mercury* to an Onion, and *Jove* himself to a Clove of Garlick. Blessed Gods are these *Ægyptian* Divinities! which they who worship devour; and which have so strong an Influence on their Votaries, that while a Man has his Gods in his Guts, he is unfit to breath in human Society.

All Cor. No *Sempronius!* No God-Eater!

1 *Cor.* Look you, my Masters, don't let these People tell *Sempronius*, that we did not shew our Breeding to them; give them a general Huzza at parting, and each of them in particular a lusty thwack o'er the Shoulders.

All Cor. Huzza!

1 *Cor.* But here comes *Coriolanus,* and in the Gown of Humility: Let us observe his Behaviour a little.

Enter Coriolanus *and* Menenius.

Men. Come, come for shame; it will be thought meer Arrogance,
T' expect the very Customs of your Country

Should

Should truckle to your Merit, and refuse
To do what all our noblest *Romans* have done.

Cor. What must I say, Sir?
A plague upon it, I can never bring
My Tongue to such a pace.   Look, Sir, my Wounds,
I got them in my Country's Service, when
Some certain of your Brethren roar'd, and ran
From the noise of our own Drums.

Men. O all the Gods! You must not speak of that:
You must desire they would think upon you.

Cor. Think upon me! Hang them!
Rather forget me, as they have done Virtue,
And every thing that's worthy.

Men. Come, come; pray speak to them in handsome
manner, and marr not your own Fortune. I must
leave you.   [*Exit*.

1 *Cit*. Now let us passing one by one salute him,
And be saluted by him, and desired
To give our Voices.
And now a Wager on the handsom'st Bow.

Cor. O *Jove*, what part am I about to play!
Here comes the beastly Crew, all Beasts alike,
Yet each a different Brute; now for their Bows,
Which will be different in them as their Looks,
Their Leers, their Sneers, their Goggles and Grimaces.
Shocking Respect! Civility offensive!
Ridiculous variety of Awkwardness!

> [*The Citizens pass by* Coriolanus, *each making a
> singular awkward Bow, and a different ridi-
> culous Grimace.*

Cor. You know the cause of my standing here?
Your Voice?

2 *Cit*. 'Tis yours noble Sir.
Cor. And yours?
3 *Cit*. Ay, ay, Sir.
Cor. And yours?
4 *Cit*. Were it as big as *Stentor's*, it were yours, Sir.
Cor. And yours?

5 *Cit*.

5 Cit. My Voice, my Lungs, and my Midriff, all are at your Service, noble Sir.

Cor. And yours?

6 Cit. Ay, by all means, Sir.

Cor. And yours?

7 Cit. Give you Joy, Sir.

Cor. And yours?

8 Cit. You shall ha't, worthy Sir

Cor. Worthy Voices.
And yours?

9 Cit. Mine, Sir, I must be paid for.

Cor. Your Price?

9 Cit. To ask it kindly.

Cor. Kindly, Sir, pray let me have it.

9 Cit. You have Wounds to shew.

Cor. Which shall be yours in private.
Your Voice, Sir? What say you?

9 Cit. Oh! Dear Sir, you have it freely.

Cor. Rare Voices! Sweet Voices! Delicate Voices!
I have your Alms. Adieu!

2 Cit. But this is something odd.

3 Cit. Foolish enough, Neighbour!

4 Cit. Very whimsical, by *Jupiter!*

5 Cit. Were it to do again —— ! But 'tis no Matter.
Come let's withdraw a little, and make room for more.

Cor. Here comes a single Voice, and by his Mien
A Tooth-Drawer, or Corn-Cutter at the best.
Death! Must I beg of him too?

1 Cit. I have not stood by, and observed for nothing.
He has flouted all my Companions, and I suppose I am
to expect the like usage in my turn; which to prevent
by *Hercules*, I'll try to mortify this haughty, doughty
Heroe.

Cor. You know what I come for, Sir.

1 Cit. O *Gemini!* Not I, by *Hercules*, Sir!
I know nothing of the Matter, Sir.

Cor. How! Not know my Business?

1 Cit. Have you Business with me, Sir? Pray what
may your Name be?   *Cit.*

Cor. My Name, Sirrah?

1 *Cit.* Nay, don't be angry, don't be angry, Sir. Some People are not willing to tell their Names. There may be Reafons, Reafons for that. But pray, Sir, what Country-man are you? When I know your Country, perhaps I may know what you come for. Are you an *Etrurian*, a *Campanian*, or a *Volfcian?*

Cor. A *Volfcian*, you Raskal?

1 *Cit.* Ay, Sir, fo I fay, Sir, a *Volfcian*; if you are a *Volfcian*, look you, you come for Cure. You have received fome Contufions, from fome *Roman* Baftinado's, and fo having heard of my Fame, do you fee, for a moft skilful Operator. There's no more to be faid, I'll do your Bufinefs, Friend, I will, by *Hercules*.

Cor. By *Jove*, you Raskal, I'll do yours.

1 *Cit.* Help! Help! Murder! Murder! What a Logerhead was I,
> [*Cit runs,* Cor. *follows beating him.*

For fetting my notable Head-piece
Againft the Great Toe of this Brawner!
> [*Exit* 1 *Cit. Enter two others.*

Cor. Here come more Voices. Sirs, your Voices, Voices.

10 *Cit.* You have deferved nobly of your Country.

11 *Cit.* You have received many Wounds for it.

Cor. I will not feal your Knowledge with the fight of them. I will make much of your Voices, and fo trouble you no farther.

Both. The Gods give you Joy, Sir, heartily.

Cor. Moft fweet Voices. Here are more of them. Your Voices? For your Voices I have fought, watched for your Voices, for your Voices, bear of Wounds two Dozen and odd; Battles thrice fix I have feen or heard of. For your Voices have done many things, fome more, fome lefs. Your Voices! Indeed I would be Conful.

9 *Cit.* And he fhall be Conful. He has done nobly, and cannot go without any honeft Man's Voice.

10 *Cit.* Therefore let him be Conful. The Gods give him Joy, and make him good Friend to the People.
All.

All. Amen, Amen! God save thee, noble Consul.

Cor. Worthy Voices! Sweet Voices! Delicate
Voices!

Enter Menenius, *with* Brutus *and* Sicinius.

Men. You have stood th' appointed time, and now
    the Tribunes
Endue you with the People's Voice, it follows
That you, invested in th' official Marks,
Anon do meet the Senate.

Cor. Is this done?

Sici. The Custom of Request you have discharg'd,
The People do admit you, and are summon'd
To meet anon, t' approve the Choice they have made.

Cor. Where? At the Senate-house?

Sici. There, *Coriolanus.*

Cor. May I change these Garments?

Sici. You may, Sir.

Cor. I'll do't without delay; and when once more
I know my self, I'll meet th'assembled Senate.

Men. I'll keep you Company. Will you along?

Brut. We here expect the People. [*Exe.* Cor. Men.

Sic. Fare you well.
He has it now; and by his Looks, methinks,
'Tis warm at's Heart.

Brut. With a proud Heart he wore his humble Weeds.
Will you dismiss the People?

Enter the Plebeians.

Sic. How now, my Masters! have you chose this Man?

2 Cit. He has our Voices, Sir.

Brut. We pray the Gods he may deserve your Loves.

2 Cit. Amen, Sir: In my poor unworthy Judgment
He mock'd us, when be begg'd our Voices.

3 Cit. Yes, certainly, he flouted us downright.

4 Cit. No, 'tis his way of Speech; he did not mock us.

2 Cit. Not one among us, save your self, but says
He us'd us scornfully: He should have shewn us
His Marks of Merit, and his Wounds receiv'd
In fighting for his Country.

Sic.

Sic. Why, did he not?

All. No, no, no Man saw them.

3 Cit. He said he had Wounds
Which he wou'd shew in private.
And with his Hand, thus waving it in scorn,
I would be Consul, says he; aged Custom
But by your Voices will not so permit me;
Your Voices therefore: When we granted that,
He said, I thank you for your Voices, thank you
For your most sweet Voices, your most delicate Voices,
Your most worthy Voices; now you have left your Voices,
You may take ev'ry thing else that belongs to you
Out of my sight. Was not this mockery?

Brut. Did you perceive,
He did solicite you in frank Contempt,
When he did want your Loves; and do you think
That his Contempt will not be grinding to you
When he hath Power to crush? Why had your Bodies
No Souls among you? Or had you Tongues to cry
Against the Rule and Dictate of your Reason?

Sic. Have you so oft e'er now deny'd the Asker,
And now on him who did not ask, but mock'd,
Bestow'd your slighted Voices?

3 Cit. He's not confirm'd; we may deny him yet.

2 Cit. And will deny him;
I'll have five hundred Voices of that sound.

1 Cit. I twice five hundred, and their Friends to help
them.

Brut. Get you hence instantly, and tell those Friends
They have chosen a Consul, that will from them take
Their Liberties, and make their Voices vile
As those of Dogs, that are as often beat
For Barking, as they are for that purpose kept.

Sic. Assemble all, and on a safer Judgment
Revoke your ignorant choice; enforce his Pride,
And his inveterate Hatred, and forget not
With what contempt he wore the humble Weed.

How

How in his Suit he scorn'd you, while your Zeal,
Dazzled and blinded by his glaring Service,
Did not discern his Insolent Deportment,
Which he most gibingly, ungravely fashion'd,
According to th' invenom'd Hate he bears you.

   Brut. But lay the fault of that on us your Tribunes;
Say, that we labour'd to remove all Scandals
That lay betwixt the Consulship and him.

   Sic. Yes, say you chose him more by our Command,
Than by the Dictates of your own Affections:
And presently, when you have got your numbers
Together, to the Capitol repair.

   All. We will so; almost all repent their choice.
Away, away, away.   [*Exeunt* Plebeians.

   Brut. Ay, now the Winds are up, and the Waves roar,
And we the Rabble wisely have enrag'd,
To be reveng'd of this *Coriolanus*;
Whom we must ruine, or our selves be lost.
This proud *Patrician* threats our new-born Pow'r,
Which either yet we must retain, or die.
So much we have enrag'd the haughty Senate,
By heading that Sedition of the People,
Which forc'd the Fathers to create us Tribunes;
And Tribunes we must be, or must be nothing.

   Sic. Then let us to the Capitol;
There let us to the best advantage guide
This Madness of the roaring Multitude,
And calm our selves; let's rule the Storm we have rais'd,
Calm as the Ruler of the raging Main,
Incensing his mad Billows to devour
Some bold Blasphemer who defies his Pow'r.

The End of the Second ACT.

A C T

ACT III. SCENE I.

Cornets. Enter Coriolanus, Menenius, Cominius, Titus
Largius, *and other Senators.*

Cor. TUllus *Aufidius* then had made new Head.
   Larg. He had, my Lord; and it was that which
Our swifter Composition.   [caus'd

Cor. So then the *Volscians* stand but as at first,
Ready, when Time shall prompt them, to make Inroad
Upon us once again.

Com. Lord Consul, they are worn and harrass'd so,
That we shall hardly, in our Age, behold
Their Banners wave again.

Cor. Saw you *Aufidius?*

Larg. On Safeguard he came to me; and did curse
Most bitterly the *Volscians*, who so vilely
Yielded the Town. He is retir'd to *Antium.*

Cor. Spoke he of me?

Larg. He did, my Lord.

Cor. How? What?

Larg. How often he had met you Sword to Sword.
That of all things upon the Earth, he hated
Your Person most: That he would pawn his Fortunes,
So he might only be proclaim'd your Vanquisher.

Cor. At *Antium* lives he?

Larg. At *Antium.*

Cor. I would I had a Cause to seek him there,
T'oppose his Hatred fully: Welcome home.

            Enter

Enter Sicinius *and* Brutus.

See where the Tribunes of the People come,
The many-headed Monsters common Tongues;
Whom I despise and hate, because the Wretches
Would raise their puny and their upstart Power
Above what we, the Nobles, ought to bear.

Sic. Pass no further.

Cor. Ha, what say'st thou?

Brut. It will be dangerous to go on, no further.

Cor. What is the Cause of this so sudden Change?

Men. Ay, what uncommon Accident has happen'd?

Com. Has he not pass'd the Nobles and the Commons?

Brut. Cominius, no.

Cor. Thou Wretch, Despite o'erwhelm thee.
What should the People do with these bald Tribunes?
On whom depending, their Obedience fails,
And grows rebellious to the greater Bench.
When not what's fit, but what must be was Law,
Then were they chosen. In a better Hour
Let what is fit, pronounce it must be fit,
And trample on their Power.

Brut. He has said enough.

Sic. He has spoken like a Traytor, and shall answer
As Traytors do.

Brut. The *Ediles,* ho. Let him be apprehended.

Enter an Edile.

Sic. Go call the People, in whose Name, my self
Arrest thee as a traytorous Innovator,
A public Foe to *Rome.* Obey, I charge thee,
And follow to thy Answer.

Cor. Hence, old Goat.

All Sen. We all will be his Sureties.

Cor. Hence, rotten thing, or I shall shake thy Bones
Out of thy Garments.

Sic. Help, help, my Fellow-Citizens.

Enter a Rabble with the Ediles.

Men. On both sides more Respect.

Sic. Here's he who would deprive you of your Power.

Brut.

Brut. Sieze him, *Ædiles.*

All Pleb. Down with him! down with him!

2 Sen. Weapons! Weapons! Weapons!

[*They all bustle about* Cor.

Men. Tribunes, *Patricians*, Citizens, what ho!
Sicinius, Brutus, Coriolanus, Citizens!
Now what will follow next? I am out of Breath,
And want the Power to speak, and they to hear.
Confusion has already taken place,
And Ruin, its Attendant, must ensue.
Patience, ye Tribunes of th' unruly People;
And thou, *Coriolanus*, too have Patience.
Speak to the People, good *Sicinius*, speak.

Sic. Hear me, People. Peace.

All Peop. Let's hear our Tribune. Peace. speak, speak.

Sic. You are about to lose your Liberties;
Marcius, by force, will seize upon your Rights,
This very *Marcius* whom you nam'd for Consul.

Men. For shame, *Sicinius*;
This is the way to kindle, not to quench.

Sen. To unbuild the City, and to lay all flat.

Sic. The City! What's the City but the People?

Pleb. 'Tis true, the People are the City.

Brut. By the Consent of all we were establish'd
The People's Magistrates.

Pleb. You so remain.

Men. And so are like to do.

Cor. That, that's the way to lay the City flat,
To bring the Roof down to the deep Foundation,
And bury all its Order, and its Beauty
In heaps and piles of Ruin.

Sic. This deserves Death.

Brut. Or let us stand to our Authority,
Or let us lose it. We do here pronounce,
In all the People's Name, in whose just Power
We were elected theirs, *Marcius* is worthy
Of present Death.

Sic. Therefore lay hold of him,

D

Bear

Bear him to the *Tarpeian* Rock, from whence
Into Deſtruction caſt him.

    Brut. Seize him, *Ædiles.*

    Cor. No; I'll die here.   *[Draws.*
There are among you who have ſeen me fighting,
Now come and try the power of this Right Hand.

    Men. Down with that Sword. Tribunes, withdraw a
      while.

    Brut. Lay Hands upon him.

    Men. Help, *Marcius,* help; ye who are Noble, help,
Both old and young.

    All Peop. Down with him! down with him!

    [The Tribunes, Ædiles, *and People are beaten in.*

    Men. Go, get you to your Houſe, begone, away,
All will be naught elſe.

    2 Sen. I pray be gone.

    Cor. Stand faſt, we have as many Friends as Foes.

    Men. Shall it be put to that?

    1 Sen. The Gods forbid.
I pr'ythee, noble Friend, home to thy Houſe;
Leave us to cure this Cauſe.

    Com. Beſides,
'Tis a Miſtake to think our Friends are equal:
So far from that, 'tis Odds ſo diſproportion'd
That Numbers cannot reach it. Come away,
For Manhood is call'd Foolery, when it ſtands
Againſt a falling Fabrick. Will you hence
Before the Rout returns? whoſe Rage grows mad
As interrupted Waters, which o'erwhelm
What they before ſupported. Come away.

                  [Exeunt Com. and Cor.

    1 Sen. This Man has marr'd his Fortune.

    Men. His Nature is too noble for the World.
He would not flatter *Neptune* for his Trident,
Nor for his Thunder *Jove*; his Heart's his Mouth:
What his Breaſt forges, that his Tongue muſt vent.
And being angry, he forgets that e'er
He heard the Name of Death.   *[Noiſe within.*

                             Here's

Here's goodly Work.

　1 *Sen.* I would they were a-bed.

　Men. I would they were in *Tyber.*
What, with a Vengeance, could he not speak 'em fair?

　Enter Brutus *and* Sicinius *with the Rabble again.*

　Sic. Where is this Viper, that would lay the City
Depopulate and bare; that he might then
Be all in all himself?

　Men. You worthy Tribunes.

　Sic. He shall be thrown down the *Tarpeian* Rock
With rigorous Hands. He has resisted Law,
And therefore Law shall scorn him further Tryal,
Than the Severity of the publick Power
Which he so much contemns.

　Men. If by the Tribunes leave, and yours, good People,
I might be heard, I then would speak one Word,
The which can be no further detrimental
Than so much loss of Time.

　Sic. Speak briefly, then,
For we are peremptory to dispatch
This viperous Traytor; for to banish him
Were to prolong our Danger, and to keep him
Were certain Death; therefore 'tis decreed,
This very Night he dies.

　Men. Now the good Gods forbid,
That our renowned *Rome,* whose Gratitude
Towards her deserving Children is enroll'd
In *Jove*'s own Book, like an unnatural Dam,
Should now devour her own.

　Brut. We'll hear no more.
Pursue him to his House, and pluck him thence;
Lest this Infection of Malignant Nature
Spread its contagious Poyson.

　Men. Hear me but one word more.
This Tyger-footed Rage, when it shall find
The Harm of thoughtless Swiftness, will too late
Tye leaden Pounds to its Heels; proceed by Process,
Lest Parties, as he is belov'd, break out,

　　　　　　　　　　　　　　　　　And

And fack great *Rome* with *Romans.*

Brut. Were that the Cafe indeed————

Sic. Can you demur then?
Have we not had a Tafte of his Obedience?
Our *Ædiles* fmit, our felves refifted? Come.

Men. Confider this; he has been bred to War,
Since he could draw a Sword, and is ill fchool'd
In boulted Language: Meal and Bran together
He throws without Diftinction. Give me leave,
And peaceably I'll undertake to bring him
Where he fhall anfwer, by a lawful Form,
Even at his utmoft Peril.
Noble Tribunes,
This is the human Way, the other Courfe
Will prove too bloody, and the End of it
Unknown to the Beginning.

Sic. Be you, *Menenius,* then the People's Officer.
Mafters, lay down your Weapons.

Brut. Go not home.

Sic. Meet on the *Forum,* we'll attend you there,
Where if you bring not *Marcius,* we'll proceed
In our firft Way.

Men. I'll bring him to you. ⎡come,
Let me defire your Company. [*to Senators.*] He muft
Or what is worfe will follow.

Sen. Come, pray let's to him. ⎡*Exe.*

S C E N E II. *The Houfe of* Coriolanus.

Enter Coriolanus *and Senators.*

Cor. Let them fet Death in its worft Shape before me,
Upon the Wheel, or at wild Horfes Heels,
Or pile ten Hills on the *Tarpeian* Rock,
That the vaft Precipice might ftretch below

The

The very Beam of Sight, yet should they find
That I am still unalter'd.

Enter Volumnia.

Sen. A *Roman* Spirit!

Cor. I wonder that my Mother
Does not approve of this my just Proceeding:
She who was wont to call them Wooden Vessels,
Things that were bought and sold for wretched Groats.
Why did you wish me milder? would you have me
False to my Nature? Rather say, I play
The Man I am.

Vol. O Sir, Sir, Sir!
I would have had you put your Power well on,
Before you had worn it out.

Enter Menenius *with Senators.*

Men. Come, come, you have been too rough, some-
You must return and mend it.   [thing too rough;

1 *Sen.* There's no Remedy,
Unless, by your Refusal, our good City
Cleave in the midst, and perish.

Vol. Pray be advis'd;
I have a Heart as much resolv'd as yours,
But yet a Brain that teaches me to use
My Anger to advantage.

Cor. What must I do?

Men. Return to the Tribunes.

Cor. Well! What then? What then?

Men. Repent what you have spoke.

Cor. To them? I cannot do it to the Gods.
Must I then do it to them?

Enter Cominius.

Com. I from the *Forum* come, and, Sir, 'tis fit
You make your Party strong, or else secure yourself
By Calmness or by Absence; all's in Uproar.

Men. Only fair Speech will do it.

Com. I think 'twill serve, if he can bend his Mind to't.

Vol. He must, he will.
Pr'ythee now say you will, and go about it.

D 3

Cor.

Cor. Muſt I go worſhip then this monſtrous Idol?
Muſt my baſe Tongue give to my noble Heart
A Lie that it muſt bear? Well, I will do it!
And yet were but my ſingle Life at ſtake,
They firſt to Duſt ſhould grind this Mould of *Marcius,*
And throw it in the Air.   Now to the *Forum;*
You have put me to a moſt unnatural Part,
Which I ſhall play moſt awkwardly.

Com. Come, come, we'll prompt you.

Vol. I pr'ythee now, ſweet Son, as thou haſt ſaid
My Praiſes made thee firſt a valiant Soldier,
To have my Praiſe for this, perform a Part
Thou haſt not done before.

Cor. Well, I muſt do it.
And thou, my Nature, and my generous Mind,
Now leave me for a while: Inſtead of theſe,
Some Harlot's wanton Soul inform my Body;
My martial Voice, that like a Trumpet, once,
Was wont to rouze up Valour in our Soldiers,
Grow ſoft and and melting as the warbling Flute,
Small as an Eunuch's Pipe, or Virgin's Voice,
That lulls aſleep a Babe: The Smiles of Knaves
Entrench my honeſt Cheeks, and may my Eyes
Grow Imitators of the falſe *Hyena*:
A Beggar's canting Tone poſſeſs my Tongue;
And my arm'd Knee, that never bow'd before,
But to the Gods and you, now bend, like his
Who has receiv'd, or who expects an Alms.
Confuſion! Muſt I do this! No, I will not:
Leſt I ſhould ceaſe to honour my own Truth;
And by my Body's Action, teach my Mind
A moſt inherent Baſeneſs.

Vol. At thy choice then,
Whether is greater Condeſcenſion, mine
To beg of thee, or thine to ask of them?
Let univerſal Ruin ſeize on all,
I laugh at Death, with as large Heart as thou.
Do as thou liſt! Thy Bravery was mine,

Thou

Thou fuck'dft it from me, but thy Pride's thy own.

Cor. Come, come, you fhall be fatisfied.
Mother, I am going to the *Roman Forum,*
Where I will cheat the Rabble of their Loves,
Decoy their Hearts, and cogg their very Souls from 'em:
Come home the very Minion of the Crowd,
The Darling of each dirty vile Mechanic.
Juft now I go, and Conful I'll return,
Or never truft my Tongue to flatter more.

   Vol. Do as you lift.   [*Exit.*

   Com. Come, come, the Tribunes wait you. Pray
           prepare
To anfwer mildly, for they're arm'd, I hear,
With Accufations ftronger than their former.

   Cor. The Word is Mildly. Pray now lead the Way;
Let them accufe me by Invention, I
Will anfwer in mine Honour.

   Men. Ay, but mildly.

   Cor. Well, mildly: Be it then mildly.   [*Exeunt.*
         Enter Sicinus *and* Brutus.

   Bru. In this part charge him home; that he affects
A Regal Power: If he evade us there,
Then urge him with his Hatred to the People,
And that the Spoil got from the *Antiats*
Was ne'er diftributed ———What, will he come?
          Enter Ædile.

   Æd. He's coming.

   Bru. How accompanied?

   Æd. With old *Menenius,* and thofe Senators
That always favour'd him.

   Sic. Have you a Catalogue
Of all the Voices that we have procur'd,
Set down by the Poll?

   Æd. I have, 'tis ready,

   Sic. Have you collected them by Tribes?

   Æd. I have, they're ready.

   Sic. Affemble prefently the People hither,
And when they hear our pofitive Decree

          D 4   Pronounc'd

Pronounc'd by vertue of their Right, then let them
Confirm it by unanimous Consent,
Insisting on their own Original Power.

Æd. I shall inform them.

Sici. When they have begun,
Let them not cease, but with a Dinn confus'd
Inforce th' immediate Execution,
Of what we chance to sentence.

Æd. Very well.

Sic. Bid them be strong, and ready for this Hint,
When we shall chance to give it.

Bru. Go about it.
Provoke him streight to rage. He has been us'd
Ever to conquer, has been still impatient
Of Contradiction: Being once chaf'd, he cannot
Be rein'd again to Temp'rance; then he speaks
What's in his Heart; and that is there, which we
Expect should break his Neck.

Enter Coriolanus, Menenius, Cominius, *with others.*

Sic. Well, here he comes.

Men. Calmly, I do beseech you.

Cor. Ye great and tutelary Gods of *Rome,*
Keep *Rome* in Safety, and the Chairs of Justice
Supply'd with worthy Men: Plant Love among you,
Adorn our Temples with the Pomp of Peace,
And from our Streets drive horrid War away.

1 Sen. Amen, Amen.

Men. A Noble Wish.

       Enter the Ædile, *and the* Plebeians.

Sic. Draw near, ye People.

Æd. List to your Tribunes, give attentive Audience.
Peace, I say.

Cor. First hear me speak.

Both Trib. Well, say. Peace, ho.

Cor. What is the Reason,
That being pass'd for Consul, with full Voice,
I'm so dishonour'd, that the very Hour
You take it off again?

                      Sici.

Sic. Answer to us.

Cor. Say then, 'tis true, I ought so.

Sic. We charge you, that you have contriv'd to take
From *Rome* all limited and lawful Power,
And to establish lawless, boundless Sway,
For which you are a Traytor to the People.

Cor. How, Traytor!

Men. Nay, temperately: your Promise.

Cor. The Fires of 'lowest Hell confound the People!
Call me their Traytor, thou injurious Tribune!
Within thy Eyes sat twenty thousand Deaths,
As many Millions in thy threatning Hands,
Both Numbers doubled in thy Lying Tongue,
Still would I dare to tell thee, with a Voice
As free as I invoke the Gods, thou ly'st.

Sic. Hear him, ye *Romans.*

All. To the Rock with him.

Sic. Silence.
We need not lay new Matter to his Charge.
What you have seen him do, and heard him speak;
Beating your Officers, cursing your selves,
Opposing Law with Force, and here defying
Those whose unquestionable Power must try him,
This Criminal, this Capital Offence,
Deserves th' extreamest Death.

Bru. But since he has serv'd well for *Rome*——

Cor. What, do you prate of Service?

Bru. I talk of that, who know it.

Cor. You?

Men. Is this the Promise that you made your Mother?

Com. Pray know——

Cor. I'll know no further.
Let them pronounce the steep *Tarpeian* Death,
Vagabond Exile, fleaing, starving, lingring
But with a Grain a Day, I would not buy
Their Mercy at the Price of one fair Word;
Nor check my Courage for what they can give,
To have it for Good-Morrow.

Sic.

Sic. For that he has,
As much as in him lies, from Time to Time,
Annoy'd, oppress'd the People, seeking means
To overturn their Power ; and now at last
Given hostile Strokes, not only in the Presence
Of dreaded Justice, but upon its Ministers ;
We, in the People's Name, and People's Power,
Even from this Instant banish him our City,
Ne'er to re-enter *Rome*, but on the Pain
Of being thrown headlong from the Rock *Tarpeian* ;
And in the People's Name, and People's Power,
We here once more pronounce it shall be so.

All. It shall be so, it shall be so ; let him away ;
He's banish'd, and it shall be so.

Com. Hear me, my Masters, and my common Friends.

Sic. He's sentenc'd ; no more hearing.

Com. Let me speak.

Sic. Speak, what ?

Bru. 'Tis now too late ; th' Offender has been sentenc'd,
And he is banish'd as a Foe to *Rome*,
And to the *Roman* People ; and it shall be so.

All. It shall be, it shall be so.

Cor. You common cry of Curs,   whose Breath I hate,
As the contagious Reek of rotten Fens ;
Whose Loves I prize, as the dead Carcasses
Of Men unbury'd, which corrupt the Air ;
I from *Coriolanus* banish you,
And here remain with your Uncertainty.
Let ev'ry feeble Rumour shake your Hearts ;
Your Enemies, with nodding of their Plumes,
Fan you into Despair ; have still the Power
To banish your Defenders, till at length,
Your Ignorance, which finds not till it feels,
Delivers you most despicable Captives,
To Foes that shall without a Blow subdue you,
And therefore scorn your City and your selves.

For

For me, thus, thus, I turn my Back upon you,
And make a better World where'er I go.

   Sic. Masters, go home; the *Ædiles* shall attend him,
And see him forth the Gates.   [*Ex. Tribunes and People*

   Cor. But here comes Company will try my Firmness;
From these my parting will not be so easy.
           Enter Volumnia, *and* Virgilia.

   Com. We must not be at this sad Enterview;
We'll meet you at the Gates.

   Cor. There I'll expect you.

   Men. Till then farewell.   [*Ex. Com. and* Men.

   Vol. O *Marcius, Marcius,* whither art thou going?

   Cor. Nay, Mother,
Where is your Ancient Courage? You were wont
To say they were Extreams that try'd Mens Spirits;
That common Chances common Men could bear.
Where are the noble Precepts that you taught me?
Those Precepts that could make invincible
The Heart that learnt them.

   Vol. Now may the red right Hand of *Jove* con-
      found
All Trades in *Rome,* and all Employments perish.

   Cor. What, what, what!
When I am wanted, I shall be belov'd.
Nay, Mother,
Resume that Spirit that was wont to say,
If you had been the Wife of *Hercules,*
Six of his Labours you'd have done, and sav'd
Your Husband so much Toil. I need not tell you,
'Tis fond to wail inevitable Strokes,
As 'tis to laugh at them. Mother, Farewell.

   Vol. Farewell my Son; I leave thee to *Virgilia,*
She has most need of Comfort.   [*Exit.*

   Cor. And thou, my dear *Virgilia*———

   Virg. Never bid me farewell, I ne'er will leave thee;
But where thou goest, thy faithful Mate will follow.

   Cor. Alas, thou talk'st of things impossible.
Can'st thou endure the hardships I must suffer?

                     Virg.

Virg. 'Tis parting, parting, is the dreadful hardſhip ;
I can bear any thing if thou art with me,
Without thee nothing.———
Alas, he hears This cold and unconcern'd!
Look, if he ſheds one pitying Tear at parting !
See, if he caſts one tender mournful Look,
Or throws one Sigh from his obdurate Heart.

Cor. Is it for me, before my inſulting Foes,
To ſhew my Grief by Tears, to mourn like Women ?
Or Men like Women: They who make me grieve
Shall feel, not ſee, my Sorrow ; they ſhall feel
The greatneſs of my Grief in my Revenge.
By all that's binding upon Earth, or awful in the Skies,
I will revenge thy Grief, and mine, *Virgilia.*
Then temperate thy Sorrow, left the Wretches
In thee, my dearer Part, inſult o'er me.

Virg. Have I the Power to moderate my Sorrow ?
Can human Nature part with all its Happineſs,
And never once complain ?

Cor. Imitate me ; compoſe, at leaſt, thy Outſide,
Suppreſs thy Sighs, tho' all within's unquiet.

Virg. As ſoon the Soul may from the Body part
Without a Groan, as I can from my *Marcius.*
Ah, how can I reſolve to part for ever ?
For ever, *Marcius,* has a fearful Sound.

Cor. Then think'ſt thou that I take my' Eternal
leave?

Virg. Thou know'ſt that to return is certain Death.

Cor. Yes, Death and Vengeance to th' accurſed Tri-
bunes.
Before yon Planet has renew'd its Orb,
I that depart from hence an empty Cloud,
Fraught with Deſtructive Thunder will return,
And break upon them with avoidleſs Ruin.

Virg. Yet my ſad Heart with doleful Beatings tells
me
We part for ever.

Cor. No ; e'er yon Moon repoints her blunted Horns,

I

I will chastize my Foes, and comfort thee.

 Virg. But whither art thou going ?

 Cor. Where I can find Revenge.

 Virg. Shall I not hear from thee ?

 Cor. Yes, if my Actions answer to my Thoughts,

The Universe shall hear from me.

 Virg. I shall be dead of Grief e'er thou return'st.

 Cor. My Mother soon will teach thee nobler Passions,

And tell thee, that my Wife should mourn like *Jove's*,

With Grief that meditates Revenge.

Now for one parting Kiss, one last Embrace.

 Virg. The last! Thou kill'st me, *Marcius.*

 Cor. Now all the Gods protect thee.

 Virg. When thou desert'st me ev'ry God forsakes me,

 Cor. Adieu !

In quest of great Revenge thy Lover flies.

 Virg. Support me, Virgins, for *Virgilia* dies. [*Exe.*

The End of the Third ACT.

ACT IV. SCENE I.

SCENE *Antium.*

Enter Coriolanus *in mean Apparel, disguis'd and muffled.*

Cor. A Goodly City is this *Antium* ; City !
'Tis I that made thy Widows ; many an Heir
Of these fair Edifices, by my Hand
Has groaning bit the Ground. Then know me not,
Left that thy Wives with Spits, and Boys with Stones
In puny Battle slay me. Save you, Sir.
Enter Citizen.

Cit. And you.

Cor. Direct me, Sir, where great *Aufidius* lies.
Is he in *Antium* ?

Cit. This very Night he holds a solemn Council,
And, at his House, he feasts our Prime Nobility.

Cor. Which is his House, Sir?

Cit. This here before you.

Cor. Thank you, Sir; farewell.   [*Ex. Cit.*
O World, thy slippery Turns! Friends now fast sworn,
Who in two Breasts now seem to wear one Heart,
Whose very Souls seem Twins, which Fate has blended
Inseparably, shall within this Hour,
On a Diffention of a Doit, break out
To bitter'st Enmity. So fellest Foes,
Whose Passions and whose Plots have broke their Sleep,
T' attempt each other's Ruin ; by some Chance,
Some Trick, not worth a Drachma, shall grow Friends
And intermix their Offspring. Who e'er thought

To

To fee the Hour when I fhould court *Aufidius,*
To be reveng'd upon ungrateful *Rome?* [*Exit.*
Mufick plays. Enter a Serving-Man.

1 *Serv.* Come, come, come, what Service is here?
Hey, where are you all? Drunk before the Guefts, by
this Light!

Enter Coriolanus.

Cor. A goodly Houfe, and fplendid Entertainment;
But I appear not an invited Gueft.

1 *Serv.* What would you have, Friend? Whence are
you? Here's no room for paltry Companions. Come
to the Door, march, march.

Cor. Juft fuch a Welcome *Coriolanus* ought
T'expect from *Volfcians.*

Enter 2 *Servant.*

2 *Serv.* Heyday, who have we here? This, by his
Garb and Mien, fhould be one of thofe Creatures whom
they call a Hanger-on, a Spunger, or Smell-Feaft.
Whence do you come, Friend? Pray, how far have
you nos'd this Supper in the Wind?

1 *Serv.* This Fellow, I'll warrant, as naturally fmells
a Supper while 'tis a dreffing, as a fagacious Hog fpies
the Wind as 'tis coming. Has the Porter his Eyes in
his Head, that he gives Entrance to fuch Companions?
Go, get you out, go.

Cor. Away. [*Strikes him.*

2 *Serv.* Away! Get you away.

Cor. Vanifh, thou Phantom, vanifh. [*Kicks him.*

2 *Serv.* I am fo horribly frighted, that I really don't
know whether I have been kick'd or no.

1 *Serv.* As certainly as I have been cuff'd, *Tony.*
We may be Evidences one for another; and fufficient
Damages we may recover. I would not part with my
Cuff for five Sefterces.

2 *Sen.* I would not give him my Kick again for ten.
But here comes *Mark,* we'll bring him into this Bus'nefs
as fure as the Day.

Enter

Enter 3d Servant.

3 *Serv.* What Fellow's this?

1 *Serv.* Hark, in your Ear, *Mark*; here is a poor Creature almoſt famiſh'd; the ſmell of this Supper has attracted the Wretch, as Loadſtone does the Iron. Now, my Maſter's Orders you know are very ſtrict, that none but the Gueſts, and their Servants, ſhould enter. This Fellow muſt be got out, d'you ſee; and be got out without roughneſs he cannot; we have tried gentle Means already. Now Roughneſs, my Friend *Tony* and I have not the Hearts to uſe, 'tis ſuch a meek, humble, good-natur'd Creature.

3 *Serv.* A Couple of Milk-Sops; let me alone.

1 *Serv.* Well, well, we leave you.

2 *Serv.* To be kick'd, *Tony*.

1 *Serv.* And cuff'd, *Pompey*: A Man ought, you know, to ſhare his Fortune with his Friend. Let us ſtep behind this Skreen, and wait the Event.

3 *Serv.* Hey, you Fellow.

Cor. Ha!

3 *Serv.* Ay, Fellow; ſo I ſay, Sir; you Fellow, you that ſtare as if you were a ſtar-gazing. What, a murrain, are we about to tell Fortunes here? I'll tell you your Fortune with a Vengeance. Do you know, my dear Friend, that ſomebody under this Roof will be kick'd immediately? Ay, ſo I ſay, kick'd, my dear Friend; kick'd for his Impudence and his Impertinence, for intruding where he had nought to do, and for provoking his Betters? Do you know this, my dear Friend?

Cor. Serve with thy Trencher, hence. [*Kicks him.*
1ſt and 2d Servants appear and laugh.

1 *Serv.* *Mark* has it as well as we.

2 *Serv.* A true Fortune-teller, by *Jove*.

1 *Serv.* Do you know, my dear Friend, that ſome Body under this Roof will be kick'd immediately?

2 *Serv.* Kick'd, for his Impudence and his Impertinence; do you know this, my dear Friend?

3 *Serv.*

3 Ser. Ah Vengeance seize you both.—— Sir, you're a most worthy, most deserving Person; and if I can do you any Service——

Cor. I want your Master, Sirrah.

3 Ser. Sir, step but into the next Room, and have a Moment's Patience till the Guests have supp'd, and I'll go up to him. Be pleas'd to walk this way, Sir.

[*Exit* Coriol.

SCENE *draws and discovers* Aufidius *and the Senators at Table.*

1 Lord. Be not so hasty, *Tullus*; stay to Night.

Auf. After your Lordships leave me, not an Hour;
The Troops are, by my Orders, march'd already,
And our Success depends on our Dispatch.
For we may likely take in several Towns
Before that *Rome*'s provided to resist us:
Whose wisest Senators have been deceiv'd,
By trusting to our late dissembled yielding;
And so disbanding hastily their Troops,
While we maintain'd, and even augmented ours,
Have naked and defenceless left their Frontiers.

2 Lord. My Lords, if my Intelligence proves true,
There is a further and a stronger Reason
Why *Tullus* should set forth without delay:
For now the Senate and the *Roman* People
Highly against each other are incens'd:
The Tribunes have Impeach'd, and mean to Try,
For Capital Offences, *Caius Marcius*,
Rome's brave Defender, and our mortal Foe.

Auf. Then, if we march while this Dissention's warm,
We bear down all before us like a Deluge;
For *Caius Marcius* was the only *Roman*,
Who, when his Country had no Army ready,
Could raise one by his Breath alone, as *Jove*
First made the World, by saying Let it be.
You may remember when in the late Dearth,
The People, mutinying, refus'd the Service,
He, in a Morning, muster'd up his Friends,

E   And

And made a terrible Incursion on us,
Which ruin'd half our Territory.

   3 *Lord. Aufidius,* thou commend'st him like a Friend.
   Auf. Life hates not Death so much as I do *Marcius,*
Yet I'll do Justice to the Worth I hate.
Even when his Country had an Army rais'd,
What was that Army when-e'er he was absent?
He was the Soul of all their warlike Enterprises.
Was it their Army that reduc'd *Corioli?*
No; 'twas the conqu'ring Arm of *Marcius* only;
Who, by that wondrous Action, lost his Name,
And found a nobler, with Immortal Glory.
Who beat the Troops which I in Person led?
Was it *Cominius, Rome's* Commander? No.
I drove *Cominius* and his Troops before me,
As Whirlwinds drive the Dust;
In Skill, in Stratagem, in Feats of Arms,
Their bravest *Romans* I surpass'd and foil'd,
Till *Marcius* came against me, like a God,
By Force divine o'er-pow'ring human Nature.
Conquest attended him where-e'er he came,
And Fortune follow'd him as Fate does *Jove.*
Where-e'er he came, Skill, Valour, Stratagem,
All in a Moment were constrain'd to yield,
Or by their Perseverance shew'd their Impotence,
And grew ridiculous.

   1 *Lord.* Perhaps the Tribunes may to Death pursue him.
   Auf. No, that, my Lords, they neither can nor dare,
For the *Patricians* are too fast his Friends:
But they eternally may disoblige him;
Which if they do, O then that we could gain him.

   2 *Lord.* I'd give, methinks, a third of my whole
      Fortune,
To see him here in *Antium* as a Friend.

   3 *Lord.* That sight would be most welcome to us all.

   1 *Lord.* To all most welcome, but most wonderful.

   Auf. Twelve times in single Combat I have try'd him,
And twelve times shamefully have from him fled.

For

For which tho' to the Death I ought to hate him,
Yet always shall my private Passions yield
To what's my Country's universal Good.
  Enter I *Servant and* Coriolanus *at a Distance; the*
   other two Servants appear at the Door.
 I *Serv.* Sir, Sir, Sir.   *[Pulling* Aufidius.
 Auf. What would the Fool have?
 I *Serv.* The Fool has earnest Business, Sir, as Fools
now-a-Days generally have; here's an odd sort of a Fel-
low that is resolv'd to speak with you, whether you
will or no.
 Auf. What's his Business?
 I *Serv.* I know not; I believe a Wager.
 Auf. Sirrah, what Wager?
 I *Serv.* I believe he has laid that he will kick your
Family round. All but your Honour have had it al-
ready.
 Auf. Sirrah, because as you're a Fool I sometimes
Have given you privilege to prate, you think
Your beastly Tongue has a perpetual Licence.
Where is this Fellow?
My Lords, I beg your Pardon for a Moment.
      [Comes to the front of the Stage.
Whence com'st thou, and what would'st thou? What's
  thy Name?
 Cor. Dost thou not know me, *Tullus?*
 Auf. No: thy Name.
 Cor. A Name unmusical to *Volscian* Ears,
And harsh in sound to thine.
 Auf. Can'st thou not speak it?
 Cor. Methinks thy Guardian Genius should inform
  thee;
Nature her self should, rouzing, take th' alarm,
And thy pure Blood, which I've so often shed,
Should swiftly to thy panting Heart retire,
And whisper there what mortal Foe is here.
 Auf. Now by the God of War there breaths but one
  Man
     E 2   Who

Who dares to talk, or dares to look like thee.
How haſt thou dar'd to appear thus here alone?
Think'ſt thou to carry *Antium* like *Corioli*,
That thou art here unſeconded, unguarded?

   Cor. 'Tis *Rome*, not *Antium*, that I come to carry.

   Auf. What ſay'ſt thou?

   Cor. Would'ſt thou revenge thy Country, or thy ſelf?
If 'tis thy ſelf thou would'ſt revenge, here ſtrike,
Ungrateful *Rome* will thank thee for the Blow.

   Auf. Ye Gods, what's this I hear!

   Cor. But if thou would'ſt revenge thy Country's
     Wrongs,
Behold me here, no common Friend to *Antium*,
No vulgar Foe to *Rome*; for I will fight
Againſt my canker'd Country, with the Spleen
Of the Infernal Furies.

   Auf. What has it done? what caus'd this wondrous
     Change?

   Cor. *Tullus*, thou ſee'ſt me here a baniſh'd Man.

   Auf. Baniſh'd! Is't poſſible!

   Cor. Hoop'd out of *Rome* by vile accurſed Slaves,
Permitted by our daſtard Nobles, who
Have all forſaken me: For which may Fortune,
And every Guardian God of *Rome* forſake them.
Tullus, I come to make a noble Barter with thee;
Give me Revenge, I'll give thee Victory.

   Auf. O *Marcius*, *Marcius*,
Each word thou haſt ſpoke has weeded from my Heart
A Root of ancient Envy. If that *Jupiter*
Should from yon glittering Firmament, in Thunder
Speak things Divine, I'd not believe 'em more
Than thee, all noble *Marcius*. Let me twine
My Arms about that Body, againſt which
My ſhiver'd Spear a hundred times has broke,
And ſcarr'd the Moon with Splinters. Here I embrace
The Anvil of my Sword, and here conteſt
As hotly and as nobly with thy Love,
As ever in ambitious Strength I did

                                 Contend

Contend againſt thy Valour. Know, thou Hero,
I lov'd the Maid I married, never Man
Sigh'd truer Breath; but, that I ſee thee here,
Thou noble Soul, more raviſhes my Heart,
Than when I firſt my wedded Miſtreſs ſaw
Paſs bluſhing o'er my Threſhold to my Bed.
Thou art arriv'd, thou Thunderbolt of War,
Even in the dreadful *Criſis* of *Rome*'s Fate.
Even now our Troops are marching, and I purpos'd
Once more to hew thy Target from thy Brawn,
Or loſe my Arm for't. Thou haſt worſted me
Twelve ſeveral Times, and I have nightly ſince
Dream'd of Encounters 'twixt thy ſelf and me:
We have been down together, in my Sleep,
Unbuckling Helms, fiſting each other's Throats,
And wak'd half dead with nothing. Worthy *Marcius*,
Had we no Quarrel elſe to *Rome*, but that
Thou thence art baniſh'd, we would muſter all
From twelve to ſeventy; and pouring War
Into the Bowels of ungrateful *Rome*,
Like a bold Deluge mark our Way with Ruin.
Let me preſent you to our Friendly Senators,
Who now to take their leaves of me are here.

    Cor. You bleſs me, Gods!   [*They go to the Table.*
    Auf. My Lords, what you have wiſh'd ſo oft in
    vain,
But what we thought no God would dare to promiſe,
Fortune and Time have of themſelves effected.
Behold the noble *Caius Marcius* here,
The Friend of *Antium*, and the Foe of *Rome*.
    All Sen. Ha, *Caius Marcius* here!   [*All riſe.*
    Auf. Baniſh'd from *Rome* by his ungrateful Country.
  1 *Sen.* Ha, baniſh'd!
  2 *Sen.* Immortal *Jupiter*!
  3 *Sen.* What Miracle is this!
  4 *Sen.* Let us bow down before the Godlike Man.
  1 *Sen.* Welcome to *Antium*; yes, a thouſand Wel-
    comes.

4 *Sen.* With you, the Tutelary Gods of *Rome,*
Are come to dwell among us.

3 *Sen.* When your ungrateful Country banish'd you
It pass'd a fatal Sentence on it self.

1 *Sen. Rome* in that Moment fell from all its Glory.

2 *Sen.* Now, in its turn, our *Volscian* State will
rise.

4 *Sen.* You come to Reign, and to Command a-
mong us.
And, if you would revenge your barbarous Wrongs
On your ungrateful Country, we have Troops
That march against it now, and good *Aufidius*
Is proud to share with you his high Commission.

Auf. Most proud of such a Partner.

Cor. My Lords, you overwhelm me with your Kind-
ness:
But my bold Hand, not Tongue, shall shew my Gratitude.

Auf. For me, I must away within an Hour,
Marcius may take a Night's Repose, and follow.

Cor. Behind you *Marcius* will not stay a moment.
Repose but feeds my inward Agitation,
While Vengeance preys upon my burning Entrails,
But Motion that will hasten dire Revenge
Will give me Ease of Mind.
By the Reception which I meet with here,
And by the Usage which I found at *Rome,*
Who would not take this *Antium* for the City
For which I all my Life had fought and conquer'd,
And *Rome* the hostile Country, of whose Natives
I, from a Boy, had made perpetual Slaughter.

Enter a Centurion.

Cent. Where is the General?

Auf. What are thy Tydings? Say.

Cent. The Troops that march'd this Evening, have
already,
Without Resistance, pass'd the *Roman* Frontiers,
And mark'd their way with Blood and Devastation.

The

'The *Roman* Territory's in a Flame,
With which the Welkin glows; th' impartial Sword
Spares neither Age nor Sex, Degree nor Order,
But makes promifcuous Slaughter of our Foes.
Confufion and Difmay feize all who efcape,
And all to their wall'd Towns for Refuge fly,
And all thofe Towns fend Poft to *Rome* for Succour.
Suffetius, your Lieutenant, begs, by me,
That you would hafte to joyn th' impatient Troops,
And take th' Advantage of their eager Fire,
And of the Foe's furprize.

Auf. To Horfe without delay. Now, noble *Marcius,*
E'er thrice the Sun his flaming Courfe renews,
Capricious *Rome* fhall curfe the fatal Hour
That e'er fhe dar'd to banifh her Defender.

Cor. I wait on you.

Auf. My Lords, we take our leaves.
May Fortune be propitious to your Lordfhips.

All Sen. Glory and Victory attend *Aufidius,*
And thee, moft noble *Marcius.*

Auf Sirrah, do you attend me to the Gate,
That you may take my Orders as I go. [*Exeunt.*

1 *Serv.* Here's an Alteration!

2 *Serv.* By *Jove,* I thought to have cudgell'd him;
and yet my Mind gave me his Cloaths made a falfe Report of him.

1 *Serv.* What an Arm he has! He turn'd me a-
bout with a Finger and a Thumb, as one would fet
up a Top.

2 *Serv.* And what a Foot he has! Well, I have
had five hundred Kicks, but never had fuch a Kick before! He mounted me like a Foot-Ball.

1 *Serv.* Well, this Frolick began with my Mafter.
This *Caius Marcius* has been us'd to Cudgel him. So
that we Servants have had an Honourable Beating.

2 *Serv.* What do you fay! Us'd to Cudgel the General!

E 4

1 *Serv.* Well Saucebox! What if I did say Cudgel the General? Did not the General say so himself? Pray what did he do before *Corioli?* Did not he Scotch him and Notch him like a Certonedo? Gad, if our General had not shewn the wrong side of himself, he might have broil'd and eaten him too.

Enter third Servant.

3 *Serv.* Oh Slaves! I can tell you News, News you Rascals.

1 *and* 2 *Serv.* What, what, what? Let us partake.

3 *Serv.* Well! I would not be a *Roman* of all Nations under the Sun, I had as lief be a condemn'd Person.

1 *and* 2 *Serv.* Ay! Why so?

3 *Serv.* Why this Offspring of *Hector* will carry my Master directly to *Rome*, and lug the Porter of *Rome* Gates by the Ears. He will mow down all before him. *Rome* will soon come into my Master's Hands. The *Romans* will be all turn'd out of their Places, and we who are Scoundrels now shall immediately become great Men.

1 *Serv.* What, we Footmen become great Men?

3 *Serv.* Why, what if we are Footmen, Puppy? How many Footmen, since I can remember, have I known preferr'd? Or Fellows worse than Footmen? Do not we see every Day a proud Splenetick Puppy lolling backwards in a Gilt Chariot; when all the Town remembers, that twenty Years ago they saw him ride behind it? I tell you, we shall be all great Men.

1 *and* 2 *Serv.* Ay, ay, we shall be all three very great Men.

3 *Serv.* But now do you know how to behave your selves, you Rascals, when you come to be great!

1 *Serv.* Not I, by *Jupiter.*

2 *Serv.* Nor I, by *Hercules.*

3 *Serv.* Then observe, and take Example by me. When I come to be a great Man, I will have but half my Memory, and no Ears at all in my Head.

1 *Serv.*

1 *Serv.* And why but half your Memory?

3 *Serv.* I will remember to mawl my Enemies, and forget to do good to my Friends.

2 *Serv.* But why no Ears in your Head?

3 *Serv.* I will have them remov'd a little nearer to my Pockets.

1 *Serv.* Whither muft that be?

3 *Serv.* Why, to the Palms of my Hands, you Scoundrel! He who fpeaks to me, fpeaks to me here.

[*Pointing to his Hand.*]

He who fpeaks to any other part of me, is an impertinent Fellow, and talks to the Deaf.

1 *Serv.* But how will you pafs your Time, when you come to be great?

3 *Serv.* Why, as that fort of great Men does who with great Fortunes have little Underftandings, and low Thoughts in high Stations. All the Morning I will be doing nothing, in fecret and in State. And while I am doing nothing gravely and myfterioufly, I will be as inacceffible, and as uncomatable, as if I were Wifdom or Honefty.

2 *Serv.* But how will you pafs your Afternoons?

3 *Serv.* Why, juft as I pafs my Mornings; in doing nothing; only I will fee a Friend or two.

1 *Serv.* What, Wits, Virtuofi, Politicians I warrant you.

3 *Serv.* No: Fools, you Puppy. Folly in Brocade fhall be my Companion, and Merit in Rags fhall be my Door-keeper. But, to pin the Basket, as foon as I come to be great, I will ufe the State as a Sharper does his Bubble, I will flatter it and cajole it egregioufly, exprefs flaming Zeal for its Service, talk of nothing but Public Spirit, and the Love of my Country; but at the fame time I will cheat my dear Country moft damnably, yet rail moft vehemently at any one who has it in his Power to cheat it more than myfelf. If I can but fill my own Coffers, I care not one Farthing if my

dear

dear Country is five hundred Millions in Debt, and Bankrupt paſt recovery.

1 Serv. Oh rare *Mark,* he has not liv'd twenty Years in the Service of great Men for nothing.

2 Serv. *Mark* has had his Eyes and his Ears open.

1 Serv. He will certainly be a very great Man.

3 Serv. Why Sirrah! I am a greater Man than you may imagine already. I am *Factotum* and *Major-Domo,* and Viceroy in my Maſter's Abſence. Look here is the Key of the Wine Cellar, Sirrah! Come, I'll begin my Reign with an Act of Grace, carry you two down into my Kingdom of Darkneſs, pierce a freſh Hogſhead, and thereby depriving you of your little Underſtandings, abſolutely gain your Affections.   [*Exeunt.*

SCENE *ROME.*

Enter the two Tribunes and Menenius.

Bru. Then you hear nothing from him?

Men. No, I hear nothing;
His Mother and his Wife hear nothing from him.

Bru. In War this *Marcius* was a worthy Officer,
But inſolent in Peace, o'ercome with Pride;
Ambitious even beyond Imagination,
And doating on himſelf.

Sic. And aiming at perpetual Soveraignty.

Men. Had *Caius Marcius* aim'd at Soveraignty
He would have been more popular.
For the *Patrician* who enſlaves this People
Muſt do it by themſelves.

Sic. We ſhould, by this, have felt his Tyranny,
To all our Sorrows, had he gone forth Conſul.

Bru. The Gods have well prevented it, and *Rome*
Sits ſafe and eaſy ſtill without him.

Enter an Ædile.

Æd. Worthy Tribunes.   There

There is a Slave, whom we have thrown in Prison,
Reports, the *Volscians*, with two several Powers,
Are entred in the *Roman* Territories,
And with the deepest Malice of the War
Destroy what lies before them.

　Bru. Go see this Rumourer whipt for his bold Lie.
The *Volscians*, whom so lately we reduc'd,
Have not the Heart to break with us.

Enter Messenger.

　Mess. The Fathers, in great Earnestness, are going
All to the Senate House; some News is come
That turns their Countenances.

　Sic. 'Tis this Slave.
Whip him before the People's Eyes, for daring
Thus to disturb the Town by his Invention.

　Mess. But, worthy Sir,
The Slave's Report is seconded; and more,
More fearful is deliver'd.

　Sic. What more fearful?

　Mess. Sir, 'tis by many Mouths deliver'd freely,
How probably I cannot tell, that *Marcius*,
Join'd with *Aufidius*, marches against *Rome*,
And vows Revenge as ample as between
The youngest and the oldest of our *Romans*.

　Sic. This is most likely!

　Bru. Rais'd only, that the weaker sort may wish
Good *Marcius* home again.

　Sic. The very Trick on't.

　Men. This is improbable, and highly so;
He and *Aufidius* are no more compatible
Than the two Branches of a Contradiction.

Enter second Messenger.

　2 Mess. You are sent for to the Senate:
A fearful Army, led by *Caius Marcius*,
Associated with fell *Aufidius*, rages
Upon our Territories, and already
Have mark'd their way with Fire, and Blood, and Ruin.

Enter Cominius.

　Com. Oh! you have made rare Work!　　　　*Men.*

Men. What News, what News?

Com. Yes, you have helpt to ravish your own
Daughters!

To see your Wives dishonour'd to your Noses.

Men. What is the News, what is the News, *Cominius?*
If *Marcius* should be join'd with *Volscians* ——

Com. If *Marcius* should be join'd ————
Why he's their God, he leads them like a Being
Made by some nobler Artist than meer Nature,
That forms Man perfecter, and shapes him better.
And under him they march with no less Confidence,
Than Heroes when commanded by a God.

Men. Oh! you have made good Work!

Com. He'll shake your *Rome* about your Ears.

Men. As *Hercules* the Pillars which he rais'd.
You have made fair Work.

Bru. But is this true, Sir?

Com. As sure as you'll look pale, and tremble too,
Before you find it other; all the Regions
With cheerfulness revolt, they who resist
Are mock'd for valiant Ignorance,
And perish constant Fools. And who can blame him?
Your Enemies and his find something in him,
Tho' you so much contemn'd him.

Men. We are all undone, unless the Godlike Man
Have Mercy equal to forgiving Gods.

Com. And who shall dare to ask it?
The Tribunes cannot do't for shame, the People
Deserve such Pity of him as the Wolf,
Does of the Shepherd: Which of his best Friends
Has not deserted him, and seem'd his Enemy?

Men. True! Were he putting to my House the Brand
Which should consume it, I have not the Face
To say, I beg you cease. You have made fair Hands:
You and your Crafts-Men, you have crafted fair.

Com. You have brought
A Trembling upon *Rome*, such as was never
So incapable of Help.

Trib.

Trib. Say not we brought it.

Men. How! Was it we? We lov'd him.
But yet, like timerous Beasts, and daftard Nobles,
Submitted bafely to your Noify Clufters,
And paffively beheld him hooted from our Walls.

Com. But they, I fear, who thus could hoot him out,
Will roar him in again. *Tullus Aufidius,*
The fecond Name of Men, obeys his Nod,
As if he were his Subaltern : Defpair
Is all the Strength, Defence and Policy
That *Rome* can make againft them.

Enter a Troop of Citizens.

Men. Here come the Clufters!
And is *Aufidius* with him! You are they
That made the Air unwholfome, when you caft
Your ftinking greafy Caps in naufeous hooting
At *Coriolanus* Exile. Now he's coming,
And not a Hair upon a Soldier's Head
Which will not prove a Scorpion.
As many Coxcombs as you threw up Caps,
He'll tumble down, and pay you for your Voices.
Nay, 'tis no Matter.
If he could burn us all into one Coal,
We have deferv'd to be confum'd together.

All Cit. Faith, we hear fearful News.

1 *Cit.* For my own part,
When I faid Banifh him, I faid 'twas pity.

2 *Cit.* And fo did I.

3 *Cit.* And fo did I. And, to fay the Truth, fo did
very many of us; nay, indeed, all of us.

All Cit. Ay, all of us.

Com. All of you fay fo! How came he banifh'd then?

1 *Cit.* What we did, we did for the beft ; and tho'
we confented to his Banifhment, yet was it againft our
Wills.   [Voices!

Com. Againft your Wills! You goodly things, you
Who urg'd you on to fuch a fatal Injury?

1 *Cit.* Why e'en our worthy Tribunes.

                                          Com.

Com. Why then your worthy Tribunes are the Persons
Who have laid waste the *Ro·ian* Territory,
Have brought their Country to the brink of Ruin,
Have to the Temples of our Gods set Fire,
Have fix'd the murthering Knife to all your Throats,
And, to the Arms of leud Licentious Ruffians,
Have given your Wives and Daughters. So farewell.

1 *Cit.* O terrible!

Com. Come on, *Menenius*, let us to the Capitol.

[*Exe.* Com. *and* Men.

2 *Cit.* Have our Tribunes done all this?

3 *Cit.* The Furies break their Necks for it.

4 *Cit.* What need we trouble the damn'd Neighbours,
for what we can do ourselves. We are the Furies.

All Cit. Ay, we are the Furies, we are the Furies.
To the Rock, to the Rock with them.

Bru. How!

Sic. What do I hear?

4 *Cit.* The Punishment they design'd for *Coriolanus*,
let them feel themselves.

All Cit. To the Rock, to the Rock with them.

Bru. Hear me, my Masters.

1 *Cit.* No, no, you have prated us into Mischief
enough already, a Plague o'your Rhetorical Throats
for it.

Sic. Can you refuse to hear us then, my Masters?

2 *Cit.* No, by no Means, but you shall take a gentle
leap first.

4 *Cit.* We shall see what a delicate Speech you'll
make when your Neck's broke.

All Cit. To the Rock, to the Rock, away with 'em.

The End of the Fourth ACT.

A C T

ACT V. SCENE I.

Enter Aufidius *and four Tribunes.*

Auf. NEver was such a Torrent of Success.
Where-e'er we march we mark our Way with
Ruin.

1 *Trib.* The *Roman* Territories are so alter'd,
So chang'd from what they were with the wild waste,
The very Natives wilder'd, lose their way;
And the Possessors of the Fertil Soil
Behold their own, and seeing it require it.

2 *Trib.* Beholding too the *Romans*, we require them.
Where are those Spirits that appear'd intrepid?
Those Spirits at whose sight our *Voscian* Troops
So often have turn'd pale with shivering Terror.

Auf. The Soul of *Caius Marcius* was the Spirit
Invigorating all; now he has left them,
The whole vast Body is become a Lump
Of lifeless and half animated Clay.

3 *Trib.* At least in *Rome* it self we thought to have
found
Some firmness; even there, on our approach,
Confusion and wild Uproar seem to lord it,
And even the Brave despair; while Peasants fly
To them for shelter, they forsake their Walls,
And wanting Firmness to expect their Fate,
Come out to meet it here.

4 *Trib.* Their very Priests rely on Heaven no more,
No more fall prostrate before *Mars* or *Jove*;
But leaving all their Temples unattended,

In

In full Procession bow the Knee to *Marcius*;
As if that *Marcius* were the only God
On whom, for their Deliverance, they depend.

Auf. Their Priests are fearful, superstitious Fools,
And proud or humble, always in excess.
But even their Heroes, and their Sages come;
Cominius and *Menenius* have been here,   [*Marcius*:
The Fellow-Conqueror one, and both the Friends of
Both bow'd their Knees,and both employ'd their Prayers,
Both cry'd for Mercy, and both cry'd in vain.

4 *Trib.* *Menenius*, by the moving Tale he told,
Of what his Country suffer'd, melted all;
But *Marcius* still remain'd unmov'd, inflexible.

Auf. Tribune, you must mistake, for I observ'd him
Look under with his Eyes, while he with Pain
Restrain'd the Moisture strugling to get free:
And much I question how he will sustain
This next and last Effort which *Rome* prepares.

3 *Trib.* What may that be?

Auf. A tender Train of mournful Ladies, with them
His Mother, and his Wife, and little Children,
Kneeling and holding up their Hands for Mercy.
Intelligence, on which I may depend,
Imports as much.   If he at last relents——

1 *Trib.* If he relents, he dies.

2 *Trib.* If he relents, this Dagger's in his Heart.

3 *Trib.* And mine.

4 *Trib.* And mine.

Auf. Away. 'Tis true, if he relents he dies,
But shall not basely be oppress'd by odds:
I, in so just Cause, alone suffice.

4 *Trib.* You! will you set your Life against a Traytor's,
And to blind Fortune trust your Country's Cause?
Suppose he kills you?

Auf. If he kills me, know
Aufidius will fall worthy of himself,
And of the Glory of his great Forefathers.
Yet for the sake of *Antium*, I'll take care

Not

Not to fall unreveng'd. But see, he comes :
I muſt receive him. To my Tent repair,
And there expect my coming.
  All. We will.   *[Exeunt.*
    Enter Coriolanus.
 Auf. Now, noble *Marcius,* what is to be done ?
 Cor. We will before the Walls of *Rome,* to-Morrow,
Set down our Hoſt. My Partner in this Action,
You muſt acquaint the *Volſcian* Lords how plainly
In all this matter I have born my ſelf.
 Auf. You have regarded them alone, have ſtopt
Your Ears againſt the general Suit of *Rome*;
Refus'd all private Whiſpers, even with thoſe
Who thought themſelves ſecure of you.
 Cor. This laſt old Man,
Who with a broken Heart went back to *Rome,*
Lov'd me above the Meaſure of a Father;
Nay, deify'd me rather. Their laſt Refuge
Was to ſend him, for whoſe old Love I have,
Tho' I to him appear'd inexorable,
Offer'd the firſt Conditions they refus'd,
And cannot now, accept to grace him only,
Who thought he could do more. A very little
I have yielded to. Freſh Embaſſies and Suits,
Nor from the State, nor private Friends, hereafter
Will I lend Ear to. Ha, what Shout is that ? *[Shout.*
Shall I be tempted to infringe my Vow
The Moment that I make it ? No, I will not.
 Enter Virgilia, Volumnia, Valeria, Y. Marcius, *with
   other Ladies and Attendants.*
 Auf. Marcius, ſee here a mournful moving Train.
 Cor. Ha, Gods ! a mournful moving Train indeed !
My Wife comes foremoſt, then the honour'd Mould
Wherein this Trunk was fram'd, and, in her Hand,
The Grand-Child to her Blood. But my Reſentment
All Bond and Privilege and Nature breaks,
And lets dull Obſtinacy now be Virtue.

      F   *Auf.*

Auf. Ay, *Marcius,* bear this great, this utmost Tryal,
And thou haft reach'd the Top of Mortal Glory.
I leave you.

Cor. Nay, *Tullus,* you muft ftay and fee ——
Auf. Excufe me;
Such Entertainments want no Standers-by,
And your Integrity to me's unqueftion'd.
I leave you to receive them.   [*Exit.*

Cor. What is that Curt'fy worth? Or thofe Dove's
        Eyes,
Which can make Gods forfworn? I melt, and am not
Of ftronger Earth than others. O for a Kifs!
Long as my Exile, fweet as my Revenge.
Now, by the jealous Queen of Love, that Kifs
I carry'd from my Love, and my true Lip
Hath ever fince preferv'd it like a Virgin.
But oh, ye Gods, while fondly thus I talk,
See the moft noble Mother of the World
Stands unfaluted; fink my Knee in Earth,
Of my deep Duty more Impreffion fhew
Than that of common Sons.

Vol. Have you forgot this Lady?
Cor. The noble Sifter of *Poplicola,*
The Moon of *Rome,* chafte as the Ificle
That's crudled by the Froft from pureft Snow,
And hangs upon the Temple of *Diana.*

Vol. This is a poor Epitome of yours,
Which by th' Interpretation of full Time
May fhew like all your felf.

Cor. The God of Soldiers,
With the Confent of fupreme *Jove,* inform
Thy Thoughts with Noblenefs, that thou may'ft prove
To Shame invulnerable, and fhew in Battel
Like a great Sea Mark, ftanding ev'ry Flaw,
And faving thofe that eye thee.

Vol. Ev'n he, your Wife, *Valeria,* and my felf,
And all this Train of noble *Roman* Ladies,
Are Suitors to you.

                                        Cor.

Cor. For any thing, except ungrateful *Rome*.

Vol. Rome, tho' ungrateful, is your Country still.

Cor. No; *Rome*, that cast me out, disown'd her
    Offspring;
And doubly I disown th' ungrateful City,
And *Volscian Antium* is my Country now:
'Tis *Antium* feeds, distinguishes, adores me,
Whereas *Rome* threw me out with basest Contumely.

Vol. I never knew the Rabble yet was *Rome*;
Yet ev'n the Rabble have reveng'd thy Cause,
Have thrown their Tribunes from the Rock *Tarpeian*,
And voted thy Repeal.

Cor. For that I thank my *Volscians*, and not them;
And I will laugh at their vile Fears, and use them
As my most deadly Foes; nay, my Revenge
Shall reach the very Walls that now protect them;
Yes, I'll destroy the very Walls that shelter them.

Vol. 'Tis a wild Vengeance,
That like an Earthquake, or a general Deluge,
Sweeps good and bad in a promiscuous Ruin:
Our noble Senators are all your Friends.

Cor. No Coward ever can be term'd a Friend,
A Coward loves himself too well to be a Friend;
And 'twas the abject Fear of the base Senate
That sacrific'd me to the Rabble's Rage;
For which, to *Volscian* Swords, and *Volscian* Fire,
I'll sacrifice their City and themselves.

Vol. Dar'st thou say this on this high Eminence,
From which thou now behold'st afflicted *Rome*,
Survey'st the awful Temples of our Gods,
That above all of *Capitoline Jove?*
Methinks I hear him from his sacred Hill
Speaking in Thunder thus; Have I decreed
That *Rome* should be my great Vicegerent here,
Should terminate its Empire with those bounds
That terminate the World; have I decreed this!
And *Marcius*, thou, dar'st thou attempt its Ruin?
And as he utters this in dreadful Tone,

Methinks

Methinks I see him o'er his sacred Temple,
Lifting above the Clouds his awful Head,
And rolling in his Red Right Hand the Thunder.

   Cor. That *Rome* should be the Mistress of the Universe,
By Sovereign Justice ne'er could be decreed;
That Revelation's but a pious Fraud,
Invented first by *Rome*'s ambitious Chiefs,
To sanctify their hourly Usurpations,
And make Injustice wear Religion's Mask.

   Vol. Oh impious!

   Cor. The Wills of Gods eternal are, like them;
And nought by Gods to Men can be reveal'd
That contradicts their great Original Will,
That contradicts great Nature's sacred Laws,
Those sacred Laws of just, and right, and fit,
Which the informing Breath of *Jove* at first
Infus'd into our new-created Souls.

   Vol. Yet still the Temples of our Gods are there,
Those Gods to whom thou hast so often sacrific'd,
The Gods of thy Fore-fathers. Can'st thou see them,
And impiously dar'st purpose to destroy them!

   Cor. 'Tis true, indeed,
There are the Temples, but their Gods are Here:
Their Gods abandon'd *Rome,* when *Marcius* left it;
And above all, the God they most adore,
Great *Mars,* the Father of their boasted Founder,
With me he went t' inhabit *Volscian* Land,
With me he marches all the toilsome Day,
With me he all the watchful Night encamps;
See where he marks his Way with Fire and Blood,
To scourge th' ungrateful *Romans!*

   Vol. What hast thou said? Thy Voice has Daggers,
     Marcius,
And thou a cruel unrelenting Soul.
Ten thousand Widows, and as many Orphans
Already has thy dreadful Vengeance made;
Destroy'd their Substance all with Hostile Fire,
And now they wander helpless, friendless, comfortless,
               And

And fill the Air with Cries and Lamentations,
Enough to pierce the Hearts of Gods and Men.
  Cor. Thanks to their Tribunes, and their noble Senate.
  Vol. From hence thou feest the Temples of our Gods:
Oh could thy Eyes but pierce the facred Walls,
And fhew thee the wild Horror that's within,
The difmal fight would break thy cruel Heart.
Proftrate before each unrelenting God,
Thou would'ft behold old venerable Age,
And helplefs Infancy, and holy Matrons,
And Virgins wither'd in their Bloom with Sorrow;
All fainting, fwooning, dying with the fear
Of what may fall to-morrow.
  Virg. Oh Gods, his Eyes their Firmnefs ftill maintain,
And we are loft for ever.
  Vol. Yet haft thou made thy Mother and thy Wife
More wretched than the miferableft *Roman*;
As thou'rt the Caufe of all this Defolation,
A Caufe that we can neither hate nor curfe,
Nor pray for thy Defeat; the reft can pray,
And they who cannot pray, yet dare to hope,
And they who dare not hope, yet dare to wifh,
And ftill are happy in th' extreameft Line.
But we can neither pray, nor hope, nor wifh;
What can we wifh for? for our Country's Triumph?
That is, alas, to wifh for thy Deftruction:
Or for thy Victory? Oh that's our Country's Ruin!
  Cor. I cannot, muft not any longer hear you.
  Vol. A little more, and I have done for ever:
Th' Ingratitude of *Rome* provokes thy Wrath
To fuch a height, that nought but its Deftruction
Can fatisfy thy thirft of dire Revenge;
And yet was e'er Ingratitude like thine?
  Cor. Ingratitude? To whom?
  Vol. To whom, but me? to me, who gave thee Life,
By whom thou cam'ft into the World a *Roman*,
Who took peculiar care t' inftruct thy Childhood,
T' inftruct thy Youth in every gen'rous Art;

                            Who

Who form'd thy growing Limbs to Martial Strength,
And steel'd thy Breast with Fortitude Divine,
Contempt of Danger, and contempt of Death,
Inflam'd thy Breast with thy dear Country's Love,
Love of great Actions and eternal Fame;
And who distinguish'd thee from other *Romans*,
As much as they're distinguish'd by the Gods
From all th' inferior Nations who surround them.
Now in requital of these matchless Benefits,
Ungrateful *Marcius* murders me.

   Cor. What means my Mother?

   Vol. And can'st thou ask? And art thou then to know
That 'tis the Maxim of each *Roman* Matron,
That when she can no longer live with Honour,
Great *Jove* aloud calls out to her to die.
And can I longer live with Honour? No;
If thou go'st on with thy curs'd Enterprize,
Death or eternal Infamy's my choice.
For I must either live to see my Country
In its last Pangs, and hear its dying Groans,
While thou, my Child, art the detested Cause,
The Subject of its frightful Imprecations;
Or live to see thee dragg'd thro' *Roman* Streets,
A dreadful Spectacle to Gods and Men,
And doom'd to die the most accursed Death
Of Traytors and of Parricides.
Therefore thou either must desist, or kill me;
This very moment thou must kill me, *Marcius*;
Here, here's the Dagger, but thou giv'st the Blow;
Yes, thou must pass o'er Her who gave thee Life,
Before thou stir'st one Step t' assault thy Country.

   Cor. What would, at last, my Mother have me do?
Must I be banish'd by the *Volscians* too?
But justly banish'd, banish'd as a Traytor?
Must I betray my Benefactors then?
Must I betray th' important Trust repos'd in me?
And so become the Out-cast of all Nations?

Vol.

Vol. I would not have thee do a shameful thing,
But love thy Glory equal with my Life ;
No ; reconcile the jarring Nations only.

   Cor. That's to betray them : They resolve on Conquest,
And will be satisfy'd with nought but Empire,
At least with Restitution of the Lands
The *Romans* so unjustly have usurp'd from them ;
That was the Treaty which *Menenius* sign'd,
And which *Rome* afterwards refus'd to ratify.
If without that Condition I desist,
How can I e'er behold *Aufidius* more ?
Or with what Eyes regard the *Volscian* Lords?
Or from the *Volscian* People what expect
But Infamy and Ruin ?   [more,

   Virg. The Gods forbid, thou e'er should'st see them
No : *Rome*, repenting of its barb'rous Usage,
Has with one Voice repeal'd its cruel Sentence.
To *Rome* with me thou surely shalt return.

   Cor. And how can I behold afflicted *Rome*,
Or how can *Rome* behold me ?
Me, who have laid its Territories waste,
Destroy'd its Cities with consuming Fire,
And made ten thousand of its bleeding Sons
Feel my remorseless Sword's devouring Edge.
If I was banish'd when I fought and conquer'd for them,
What can I now expect but certain Death
From its tumultous, feeble, faithless Tribunes ?
Not only my Revenge, my Preservation
Requires that *Rome* should fall. Can you desire
Your Son should die to save his mortal Foes ?
No : Perish, perish this ungrateful City !

   Vol. Dye then, *Volumnia* : But, before I die,
Thus, thus the Mother falls at the Son's Feet,
Not to ask any Pity for her self,
But Mercy, Mercy, for her sinking Country.
Down, Ladies, down.

F 4

Cor.

Cor. Oh, the confusion of my tortur'd Soul!

Vol. Pronounce *Rome* safe, or I am fall'n for ever.

Cor. Ye Gods, ye Gods! live *Rome*, and *Marcius* die
first.

Oh, rise, my Mother; you and *Rome* have conquer'd;
But your unhappy Son's for ever lost.
Hoa! Who waits there?
Give Orders that the Troops return tow'rds *Antium*,
And tell *Aufidius* I expect him here.
The Troops march back towards *Antium*, where must
I go?

Virg. Once more with us to *Rome* thou shalt return.
Thy Apprehensions to the Winds deliver.
Our *Romans* will regard thee as a God,
For shewing Mercy to thy bleeding Country,
After such mortal Provocations giv'n
By black Ingratitude, and base Injustice.

Vol. Thou hast done a Godlike Deed, and supream
Jove,
And ev'ry God who sees it, will reward it.

Virg. Thou'st rais'd up a whole miserable People,
All in a moment, from Despair to Rapture.

Vol. Oh, the transporting Joy that we shall meet
At our Return in ev'ry Voice and Eye!

Virg. Our greatest Conquerors were ne'er receiv'd
With half the Joy, with half the Acclamations!

Vol. Then what must our tempestuous Raptures be!
Oh, we are happy as the Deathless Gods!
Nor shall our Triumph be confin'd to *Rome*,
Or the short Time we live.

Virg. No: o'er the Universe its Fame shall spread.

Vol. Nations unborn, and Languages unform'd
Shall tell the blissful Tale, and bless the Actors.
Yes, with Immortal Bliss, Immortal Fame——

Virg. And everlasting Love we shall be crown'd.
Blest with the long Possession of my *Marcius*,
I ne'er till Death will part with him again.

Cor. Here cease your Transports. See, *Aufidius* comes:
Please

Please to retire to yonder Tent a while,
For I must take a long but fair Adieu.   [*Ex. Women.*
Enter Aufidius.

Tullus Aufidius. Ha!
Why dost thou greet me with this alter'd Countenance,
This silent Wonder in thy wrathful Eyes?

  Auf. Just now a Slave brought Orders to the Troops
That they should backward turn their March to *Antium*;
And impudently said he came from you.

  Cor. 'Tis true, I sent him.

  Auf. Then, *Caius Marcius*, you have done much
        Wrong
To me, and all the *Volscians*.

  Cor. O *Tullus*, *Tullus*, hadst thou but been by
To hear the piercing things that mov'd my Soul,
Thou would'st have sworn they might engage even
        Jove
To change his high Decrees.

  Auf. Your Mother and your Wife we know have
        done this.

  Cor. The noblest Mother, and the tender'st Wife!

  Auf. Yes, they are dear Relations, I confess,
And 'tis for them you set at Scorn the Gods,
By whom so solemnly you swore.

  Cor. Unlawful Oaths are in themselves invalid.
And is it lawful to destroy my Country?

  Auf. No, not your Country, but your mortal Foes;
And so the *Romans*, by their barb'rous Usage,
You said were grown: You said, and spoke the Truth;
And this is but a poor and mean Evasion,
And you must answer 't to th' Avenging Gods,
By whom you swore with bitter Imprecations.

  Cor. Then I will answer it; let that suffice;
And to the Gods alone I'll be accountable.

  Auf. Yes, I dare trust them, soon they will revenge
The Wrong that's done to their Almighty Powers:
But you must answer your Offence to me.

  Cor. To you!

Auf.

Auf. To me, ungrateful Man.
Who took you in, with open Arms, but I,
A supplicating Exil and a Vagabond,
Fallen below Pity, nay below Contempt?
Who gave his Honour to the *Volscian* Lords,
That you inviolably should be theirs?
And rais'd you up to more than former Glory,
And even to envied Greatness, to the Power
Of taking a Revenge as ample as thy Wish?
Now what's the great Return you make for this?

Cor. Such a Return as none but I could make;
Such a Return as, not ten Days ago,
Would have been Phrensy in the proudest *Volscian*
To hope, or to expect.
I infus'd Spirit thro' your abject Troops,
Gave them a Taste of Deathless Victory,
First shew'd them that the *Romans* can be conquer'd:
Compell'd my Countrymen to sue for Peace,
And sign an ignominious Treaty with you;
The same Conditions which *Menenius* brought;
Shameful for them, but glorious to your Troops,
And advantagious to the *Volscian* State.

Auf. Name not the faithless Treaty, that condemns
    you;
For to what serves it, but to give *Rome* Breath
To recollect her self, and pour Revenge
Into the very Heart of *Volscian* Land?
Doing no more, thou hast done less than nothing,
But rankled and envenom'd more a Foe
Too much provok'd by cursed Pride before.

Cor. How selfish Men stalk under public Zeal
To their base Ends! Before this Peace was granted
Thou wert not satisfy'd, but to thy Followers
Thou breath'dst, in Corners, sullen Discontent.
Then I went on too fast, and too precipitate,
And left whole Fortresses and Towns behind me,
With an Intention to betray the *Volscians*,
By cutting off their Intercourse with *Antium*.
'Tis not too little, but too much Success,   That

That thus provokes the great *Aufidius*' Envy.

Auf. Envy a Traytor and a Parricide!

Cor. Thou say'ft that I have Obligations to thee;
To them thou oweft that thou fpeak'ft this, and liv'ft.
Yes, take thy Life; *Jove* gave it thee at firft,
I give it now; and now I owe thee nothing.

Auf. My Life from you! Firft have it in your Power.

Cor. Thou know'ft, *Aufidius*, 'tis much harder for me
To fay I'll kill thee, than to ftrike the Blow.
Twelve times, thou know'ft, when I advanc'd my
    Sword
The Deftinies advanc'd their fatal Sheers,
And nought but ignominious Flight could fave thee.

Auf. And canft thou think thou art the Man thou
    wer't,
When thou retain'dft thy Honour and thy Virtue?

Cor. Both Gods and Men, with one Confent, proclaim
That *Marcius* is the Man he always was;
His Honour and his Virtue ftill the fame:
And therefore the Immortal Powers affift me,
And Fortune is my Friend and my Confed'rate,
And whatfoever Side I chufe, for that declares
'Tis I that made my foaring Country ftoop,
That never ftoop'd before; and when they fu'd
For Peace, to me they fupplicating fu'd,
And took no Notice of the Great *Aufidius*.
Now try the Voices of thy Countrymen;
I gave them Orders to march back to *Antium*,
See then if thou can'ft lead them on to *Rome*.

Auf. Too well I am convinc'd thou haft feduc'd,
By curfed Flattery, and by fhameful Arts,
My Followers, my Soldiers, and my Friends.

Cor. 'Tis likely I fhould ftoop to flatter *Volfcians*,
Who ne'er could bow my Nature to Compliance
Even with my Country's mean and abject Cuftoms.
'Twas my Authority alone feduc'd them,
Authority from Deathlefs Actions drawn,
And from my Triumphs o'er their baffled Leader.

                                            Auf.

Auf. Oh, they muſt needs admire the wondrous Man,
Who for ſome certain Drops of Womens Rheum,
That are as cheap as Lies, betray'd and ſold
The Labour of their Noble Enterprize,
Their Intereſt, and their Glory.   [Nature,

Cor. Thus far I've ſtruggling curb'd my impatient
But on thy Life no more; for, by great *Mars*———

Auf. Name not the God, thou Boy of Tears.

Cor. Nay then ———

Auf. Upon this Spot. retract thy injurious Order,
Or thou ſhalt ſeal it with thy Blood, or mine.

Cor. Then take thy Wiſh.
This Boy, that, like an Eagle in a Dove-Court,
Flutter'd a thouſand *Volſcians* in *Corioli*,
And did it without Second or Aſſiſtance,
Thus ſends their mighty Chief to rail in Hell.

                        [*Fight*, Aufid. *falls.*

Auf. O *Marcius!* thou haſt conquer'd, and *Aufidius*
Is now but Duſt; but, with my flowing Blood,
My Frantic Paſſion cools; forgive me, *Marcius*,
That I thus far provok'd thy noble Nature:
And I, to merit thy Forgiveneſs, tell thee
That thou, like me, art in the Shades of Death,
And ſoon wilt follow me, unleſs thou --- Oh!   [*Dies.*

Cor. Hail! and eternally Farewell, brave *Tullus!*
But what's the Caution Death thus interrupted?
Thou ſoon ſhalt follow me, unleſs thou --- what?
Oh! here's the Explication of th' Ænigma.

Enter three of the Tribunes, with their Swords drawn.

1 *Trib.* Where is our General?

Cor. There.

1 *Trib.* What Wretch's Hand has done this curſed
                        Deed?

Cor. A Wretch whoſe Hand's inur'd to *Volſcian* Blood.
Then love thy ſelf, and vaniſh. Go, be gone,
Provoke him not.

1 *Trib.* Provoke the Villain!
I come not only to provoke but kill him.

                                        Cor.

Cor. If thou haſt Power to kill him, he'll engage
To own that he's a Villain. This to try. [*Kills him.*
So, for all thee I ſtill am very Honeſt.

2 Trib. Our fourth Man either loyters, or betrays us.
Let us ſtrike home, and let us ſtrike together.
We will revenge our General and our Friend.
What, do you recoil?

Cor. Yes, like a Martial Engine, to advance
With certain Execution. Lie thou there.
[*Kills the ſecond. Women ſhriek behind the Scenes.
Enter fourth Tribune.*

Vol. and Vir. Behind, Oh, look behind.

Cor. The Women ſee and ſhrick. I muſt diſpatch.
Theſe two are Victims to my juſt Reſentment,
Fall thou a Sacrifice to *Tullus*'Ghoſt
[*Kills the 3d Trib. and the 4th runs him thro' the Back.*

4 Trib. Now falls the Sacrifice which moſt will pleaſe
him. [*Loud Shriek.*

Cor. No, treacherous Villain, I have Life remaining
To ſend thee to the under World before me,
And thou ſhalt be the Lacquey of my Fate.
Fly, Dog, and tell *Aufidius* that I come. [*Falls.*
Enter Volumnia, Virgilia, *and* Valeria.

Vol. Alas, my Son, my Son!

Vir. My deareſt Lord!
Ah, Gods, the Blood runs ſtreaming from his Wound!
He bleeds to Death! and is no Succour nigh?
Haſte, fly for help.

Cor. All Help is vain, for we muſt part, *Virgilia.*

Vir. No, we muſt not; there's not a God in Heaven
So cruel to decree me quite ſo wretched.

Cor. My Blood and Life are at the loweſt Ebb.

Vir. Ah, now I ſee a Sight that will diſtract me,
And dread the utmoſt Malice of my Fate;
For the firſt time my *Marcius* now turns pale.

Vol. Yet looks undaunted ſtill.

Cor. Mother, farewell. Nay, if you weep!——

Vol. 'Tis I have only Cauſe, 'tis I have done this,
Thy

Thy filial Piety has been thy Fate;
And I have kill'd my Son.

 Cor. You have fav'd your Country.

 Vol. What's my Country now,
To me a Widow, helpless, childless, comfortless?

 Cor. My everlasting Fame be now your Son,
And your own Deathless Glory be your Husband.
Where-ever *Roman* Annals shall be read,
The Godlike Action you have done this Day
To endless Ages will transmit your Name,
And all the Good eternally will bless you.
Be it your Care to comfort poor *Virgilia.*

 Vir. Is this the Happiness that I expected?
Now first I hop'd to have thee mine entirely,
Inseparably mine, and now we part,
For ever part. And must we? No, we will not;
For when thou go'st *Virgilia* will not stay.

 Cor. Virgilia, let me die as I have liv'd,
And, like a *Roman,* view the Tyrant Death,
With Scorn, as I have always done in Battle.
Thy Grief alone can make him formidable,
One parting Kiss, a long, a long Farewell. [*Dies.*

 Vir. He's gone, he's gone, and I no more must see
   him!
No more must dwell upon his charming Tongue,
And hang on his enchanting Lips no more.
And thou prophetic Vision of the Night,
And ye the dire Forebodings of my Soul,
All, all is come to pass. See here he lies:
Ay, here he lies, surpriz'd, surrounded, murther'd.

 Vol. Yet in his Fall he still is *Coriolanus,*
Himself alone a Conqueror o'er Numbers;
Himself the dread Revenger of his Murther.
But the just Gods require an ampler Vengeance,
For their lov'd Heroe's Death. Even now the Years
Come crouding on, for so the Gods inspire me,
When *Rome* shall all the Land around possess,
And even the Name of *Volscian* be no more. [*Shout.*
            Enter

Enter Cominius, Menenius *and Attendants.*

My Lords *Cominius* and *Menenius* here!

Com. We came with fresh Instructions from the
Senate,
And larger Offers still of shameful Peace,
But find the *Volscians* fled in wild Confusion,
And panic Fright, for so our Hinds inform us;
Upon what wondrous Accident they know not.

Vol. See there the Cause;
See where their mighty Chief, *Aufidius*, lies.

Men. And, Oh! see *Marcius* pale in Blood beside
him.

Com. What provok'd Death to make this dismal
Havock!

Vol. That Question must redouble all my Griefs:
I was the fatal, I the only Cause.

Com. You?

Vol. I, on my Son, prevail'd at length for Mercy;
Which caus'd *Aufidius* Rage, and all their Fates.

Com. O Death! thou hast a costly Conquest made,
And wasted all at once, like foolish Spendthrifts,
The Soil that would have brought thee many a plen-
teous Harvest.
Tho' *Marcius* fill'd his Country with Confusion,
Which still lies strugling in Convulsive Pangs,
He shall not pass unprais'd nor unlamented:
For 'twas thy Fate in Death, as in thy Life,
To be thy Country's Champion and Deliverer.
  In solemn, slow Procession let us march,
And bear the sad Remains of him to *Rome*,
Where pompous Rites of Funeral shall be paid them.
Where, Ladies, you who have thus nobly sav'd
Your Country, shall receive immortal Honours.
But they who thro' Ambition, or Revenge,
Or impious Int'rest, join with foreign Foes,
T' invade or to betray their Native Country,
Shall find, like *Coriolanus*, soon or late,
From their perfidious Foreign Friends their Fate.

F I N I S.